Acting Edition

Pirandello
and Other Plays

by Don Nigro

Copyright © 2021 by Don Nigro
All Rights Reserved

PIRANDELLO AND OTHER PLAYS is fully protected under the copyright laws of the United States of America, the British Commonwealth, including Canada, and all member countries of the Berne Convention for the Protection of Literary and Artistic Works, the Universal Copyright Convention, and/or the World Trade Organization conforming to the Agreement on Trade Related Aspects of Intellectual Property Rights. All rights, including professional and amateur stage productions, recitation, lecturing, public reading, motion picture, radio broadcasting, television, online/digital production, and the rights of translation into foreign languages are strictly reserved.

ISBN 978-0-573-70942-5

www.concordtheatricals.com
www.concordtheatricals.co.uk

FOR PRODUCTION INQUIRIES

UNITED STATES AND CANADA
info@concordtheatricals.com
1-866-979-0447

UNITED KINGDOM AND EUROPE
licensing@concordtheatricals.co.uk
020-7054-7200

Each title is subject to availability from Concord Theatricals Corp., depending upon country of performance. Please be aware that *PIRANDELLO AND OTHER PLAYS* may not be licensed by Concord Theatricals Corp. in your territory. Professional and amateur producers should contact the nearest Concord Theatricals Corp. office or licensing partner to verify availability.

CAUTION: Professional and amateur producers are hereby warned that *PIRANDELLO AND OTHER PLAYS* is subject to a licensing fee. The purchase, renting, lending or use of this book does not constitute a license to perform this title(s), which license must be obtained from Concord Theatricals Corp. prior to any performance. Performance of this title(s) without a license is a violation of federal law and may subject the producer and/or presenter of such performances to civil penalties. Both amateurs and professionals considering a production are strongly advised to apply to the appropriate agent before starting rehearsals, advertising, or booking a theatre. A licensing fee must be paid whether the title(s) is presented for charity or gain and whether or not admission is charged. Professional/Stock licensing fees are quoted upon application to Concord Theatricals Corp.

This work is published by Samuel French, an imprint of Concord Theatricals Corp.

No one shall make any changes in this title(s) for the purpose of production. No part of this book may be reproduced, stored in a retrieval system, scanned, uploaded, or transmitted in any form, by any means, now known or yet to be invented, including mechanical, electronic, digital, photocopying, recording, videotaping, or otherwise, without the prior written permission of the publisher. No one shall share this title(s), or any part of this title(s), through any social media or file hosting websites.

For all inquiries regarding motion picture, television, online/digital and other media rights, please contact Concord Theatricals Corp.

MUSIC AND THIRD-PARTY MATERIALS USE NOTE

Licensees are solely responsible for obtaining formal written permission from copyright owners to use copyrighted music and/or other copyrighted third-party materials (e.g., artworks, logos) in the performance of this play and are strongly cautioned to do so. If no such permission is obtained by the licensee, then the licensee must use only original music and materials that the licensee owns and controls. Licensees are solely responsible and liable for clearances of all third-party copyrighted materials, including without limitation music, and shall indemnify the copyright owners of the play(s) and their licensing agent, Concord Theatricals Corp., against any costs, expenses, losses and liabilities arising from the use of such copyrighted third-party materials by licensees. For music, please contact the appropriate music licensing authority in your territory for the rights to any incidental music.

IMPORTANT BILLING AND CREDIT REQUIREMENTS

If you have obtained performance rights to this title, please refer to your licensing agreement for important billing and credit requirements.

TABLE OF CONTENTS

Pirandello 1
The Recollection of Green Rain 73
Pinocchio 89
Rusalka 102
Humpty Dumpty 113
Brimstone Run 123
Nictzin Dyalhis 131

Pirandello

A Play

by Don Nigro

CHARACTERS

IL DUCE
PIRANDELLO
THE ACTRESS
THE WIFE
THE FATHER-IN-LAW
THE DAUGHTER
THE MISTRESS

SETTING

The stage of a theatre late at night. A table and chair where Pirandello sits writing. Fragments of set and props scattered about the stage. Pieces of furniture. Other chairs and tables. A bed. An old oval mirror. A number of step units arranged rather haphazardly, a bit like the rough draft of an Escher print of stairways to nowhere.

"There reigned...during these vertiginous moments that fascination of the monstrous, that temptation of the horribly possible..."
– Henry James, *The Golden Bowl*

"He is but mad yet, madonna; and the fool shall look to the madman."
– Shakespeare, *Twelfth Night*. Act One, Scene Five.

"And Love said to the old man, I will leave you now."
– Lord Dunsany

(The stage of a theatre. Night. Furniture and props scattered about, and step units here and there. **PIRANDELLO** *sits at a table, writing in a small circle of light.* **IL DUCE** *moves out of the shadows, looks out into the greater darkness of the auditorium.)*

IL DUCE. So, you do this a lot, do you? Stay after the play is over and sit here alone on the stage?

PIRANDELLO. I like to write here. It's quiet, and I enjoy the illusion of safety, surrounded by the darkness. An empty theatre is a kind of holy place.

IL DUCE. I'd think you'd get lonely here all by yourself, in the middle of the night.

PIRANDELLO. Writing is a lonely profession. When I feel the need for company, I talk to the ghosts. Theatres have the best ghosts. It's like living in your own private doll house. When you're safe inside, you can make up anything you want. You can have a dialogue with anybody, living, dead or imaginary. You can share dirty jokes with God if you like.

IL DUCE. I imagine God would be quite lonely, too. I mean, what does he have to do all day, besides killing people? Play checkers with the Devil? Of course, they're most likely the same person, talking to himself in the mirror. I imagine playwrights tend to see themselves as God looking in the mirror.

PIRANDELLO. I don't think I'd want to be God.

IL DUCE. Of course you want to be God. Everybody wants to be God. Except for God, who probably wants to be Mussolini.

(Practicing heroic poses in front of an old oval mirror.)

Pretty good looking guy, aren't I? Do you know that people actually used to call me ugly? Nobody says that any more. I guess I got better looking with age. Also, all those people are dead. Not that I killed them. Well, not all of them. I might have hanged some of them. What fun is it being a dictator if you can't hang up your enemies like Christmas decorations? It's dark in here. Can't we have more light? I can't see myself properly.

PIRANDELLO. *(Calling up into the darkness at the back of the house.)* Garibaldi? Are you still here? Il Duce wants more light.

IL DUCE. Garibaldi? You've got Garibaldi in your light booth?

PIRANDELLO. Our jack of all trades. Nobody can remember what his real name is. We call him Garibaldi because he has a beard and a great sense of dignity and is very stubborn and whenever anybody goes looking for him he's always someplace else.

IL DUCE. Well, he seems to have left the building tonight.

(Abruptly, more lights come up. Pools of light here and there mixed with shadow and latticework patterns.)

PIRANDELLO. There he is. Good man, Garibaldi. Thank you.

IL DUCE. I think he's actually made it darker.

PIRANDELLO. He must be fiddling with the light settings for the dream scene. There is a scene in this play in which the protagonist, who's a famous playwright, is alone in the theatre late at night when –

IL DUCE. Did you hear that?

PIRANDELLO. What?

IL DUCE. Listen.

PIRANDELLO. I don't hear anything. It's probably just Garibaldi, scuttling around up there.

IL DUCE. It sounded like owls.

PIRANDELLO. Owls?

IL DUCE. Lately I keep hearing owls.

PIRANDELLO. I don't think we have any owls. We have rats. Theatres are full of rats and actors. We used to have pigeons in the attic, but the rats ate them. I think it was the rats. It might have been the actors.

IL DUCE. I don't trust pigeons. They're always muttering behind my back and shitting on my statues. But I've been hearing owls at the oddest times. Just before I drop off to sleep. In the shower. While evacuating my bowels. I don't mean that I evacuate my bowels in the shower. I hear owls while evacuating my bowels, and in the shower, and sometimes at the moment of orgasm. And my mind's been playing tricks on me. I wake up and don't know where I am. It's like trying to remember a dream. You reach out to catch hold of it but it's just disappearing around a corner. I'm actually having a moment like that right now. Why am I here?

PIRANDELLO. I don't know. Is that a philosophical question, or –

IL DUCE. It's incredibly frustrating, like going into a room and not being able to remember what you went in there for. Wait. I've got it. I come bearing good news. I'm here to inform you that you've been selected to have the tremendous honor of writing the authorized biographical play about my life. I know you must be thrilled. You are thrilled, right? You don't look like you're thrilled. Why aren't you thrilled?

PIRANDELLO. Well, it is a great honor, of course, that you would entrust me with a task of such importance, but you know, I don't really –

IL DUCE. You don't really what?

PIRANDELLO. I tend to write plays about identity and the elusive nature of reality. I'm probably not the best person to write about somebody who knows exactly who he is and is so certain about everything.

IL DUCE. How do you know what I'm certain of?

PIRANDELLO. I just mean that you always seem to be so confident about –

IL DUCE. So you don't want to write a play about my life?

PIRANDELLO. It's not that I don't want to. I just feel that my particular, rather modest abilities –

IL DUCE. You think it's beneath you?

PIRANDELLO. Absolutely not. But a playwright can't necessarily always just sit down and crank out a play because somebody tells him to.

IL DUCE. Of course you can. If I walked into a restaurant and ordered a pizza, you'd make me a pizza. I walked into a theatre and ordered a play. You're a playwright. Make me a play.

PIRANDELLO. But my plays are about the ambiguities involved in believing we know the true nature of reality, when in fact it's not at all clear that –

IL DUCE. How about if we chop off your dick? Would that be real enough for you?

(Pause.)

Relax. I'm joking. Well, sort of. Although it's amazing how effective threatening to cut off somebody's dick can be in resolving their questions about the nature of reality. But no pressure. I'm actually a very sensitive, artistic sort of fellow. I play the violin and love opera. Really. I like nothing better than listening to fat people howling at each other and pretending to die while wearing silly hats. I listen to *Pagliacci* over and over until my ears bleed. And I'm also an actor. I play the part of Il Duce. I wear a mask. But when I take my mask off, my face comes with it, and there's nothing left but a grinning skull. Or just an empty space, like the Invisible Man. Except for a nose. I might just be a nose, floating in the void.

(Among the scattered props, he spies a violin.)

Look. A violin. Is there a violin in this play?

PIRANDELLO. Garibaldi's been cleaning out the prop room.

IL DUCE. Would you like to hear me play *Pagliacci* on the violin?

PIRANDELLO. Well, of course, ordinarily I would very much, but I really need to finish this –

IL DUCE. *(Playing, very, very badly, on the violin, a bit of Pagliacci.)* Pretty good, huh?

PIRANDELLO. I've never heard anything quite like it.

IL DUCE. You had no idea I was so talented, did you?

PIRANDELLO. You're obviously an extremely gifted person.

IL DUCE. Horse shit. That sounded like a raccoon fucking a chicken. Don't kiss my ass. My ass is chapped from everybody and his brother kissing it. All day and half the night all over Italy people are standing in line to kiss my ass. At first it was actually rather enjoyable, but my ass is only human, and even a great man's ass can only stand so much slobbering all over it. All I do is make a little joke about cutting off somebody's dick and the next thing I know their lips are glued to my ass like the suction cup of an octopus. What I can really use is somebody brave enough to tell me the truth.

PIRANDELLO. But what is truth?

IL DUCE. Truth is whatever sort of crap I can get some dumb son of a bitch to swallow. Truth is not about truth. Truth is about power. You can get people to believe any damned crock of shit, however ridiculous, as long as it's what they want to hear, and you just keep screaming it over and over. People actually like being led around like sheep. That way they don't have to go to the trouble of using their brains, which can be very depressing.

PIRANDELLO. Not always.

IL DUCE. So you actually use your brain?

PIRANDELLO. I'm a writer. I have no choice.

IL DUCE. And are you depressed?

PIRANDELLO. Yes, but –

IL DUCE. I rest my case. But I shouldn't have joked about cutting off your dick. You're probably going to need it at some point or other. I mean, you have a wife, don't you? She's probably going to need it. Although I heard a rumor she's crazy, and you've taken up with an actress who's half your age. Between the two of them, they must keep you pretty busy. Is there any truth to that?

PIRANDELLO. Too much and also not enough.

IL DUCE. An answer which doesn't actually mean anything. Just the sort of playwright I need. A master of ambiguous bullshit. So, when you write this play about me, make me heroic, but humble. Fierce, but kind to puppies. Godlike, but as pure as the girl next door. Can you do that? They gave you the Nobel Prize. You must be good at something.

PIRANDELLO. Unfortunately, creation doesn't usually work like that. At least, not for me.

IL DUCE. I'm not asking you to create the goddamned universe. I just want you to write a play. Incredibly stupid people do this all the time.

PIRANDELLO. But creating a work of art really is like creating a universe. Or giving birth.

IL DUCE. My mother almost died when I was born. I had a head the size of a watermelon. They could hear her screaming all the way to France. Is it like that when you write?

PIRANDELLO. Well, not quite that painful, usually, but it is like bearing a child, in the sense that just wanting to get pregnant doesn't make it happen. A mysterious conjunction must take place. A kind of chemical reaction in one's head. And suddenly, you don't know how or why, there's something flowing out of you onto the paper faster than you can write it down. There are things you can do to make it more likely to happen, but you can't force it.

IL DUCE. You can if you want to keep peeing standing up. Now I'm frightening you again. Good. But I'll make you a deal. I promise not to cut off your dick. Whether you write a play about me or not, you get to keep your dick. Is that magnanimous of me, or what?

PIRANDELLO. Thank you. I really appreciate that.

IL DUCE. What am I supposed to do with a playwright's dick, anyway? I'm just presuming you even have a dick. Maybe instead of cutting off your dick, I could just shoot you in the elbow. Is that fair? And don't tell me a great man like myself wouldn't stoop to shooting a playwright in the elbow. I'm Il Duce. It's my duty to shoot people in the elbows. And if you can't write without your elbow, I can get D'Annunzio to write a play about me. D'Annunzio has kissed my ass so many times, his mustache smells like dog shit. Not that I've spent a lot of time smelling D'Annunzio's mustache.

But I have stepped in a lot of shit. Politics is a dunghill, and I am the cock who crawls to the top and crows. Who said that? Did I say that? Am I quoting myself again? I don't even know any more.

PIRANDELLO. Isn't D'Annunzio dead?

IL DUCE. That would depend on what year this is, and unfortunately I left my sundial in my other pants. Anyway, what's your point? Shakespeare is dead, but people still do his plays.

PIRANDELLO. Yes, but those are plays he wrote when he was alive. Even Shakespeare was not as prolific after he was dead.

IL DUCE. That's not my fault. I didn't kill him. The truth is, violence doesn't make me nearly as happy as it used to. I didn't even want to get into this war. The English made me do it, with their buck teeth and ugly little dogs. And I warned Hitler not to invade Russia. What kind of an imbecile invades Russia? You freeze off your balls, and then the bears eat you. But would he listen? That crazy little fart. Sometimes I get so frustrated I just want to strip off my clothes and roll in the mud like a pig. My wife is always nagging and my mistress is always weeping. Between the two of them, I almost prefer the Germans. When I was a boy I told myself, some day I will live in a big golden tower and fornicate with everybody's daughter. I will make fornication great again! And I'll be the smartest person in the world because we'll make sure everybody else is stupid. I will make ignorance great again! People who've just met me sometimes get the impression I'm not very bright. This is something a person can use to his advantage if he plays his cards right. But the best thing is if everybody is just shit-in-their-pants scared of you. This is what I learned at school: when somebody punches you in the head, grab the scissors and stab him in the throat. Don't let anybody get away with anything. Of course, maybe that's why I have no friends. I have plenty of people who want me to think they're my friends, either because they're stupid or they're afraid I'm going to kill them. But why do I need friends? There's only two kinds of people: the strong and the weak. The strong lead. The weak follow. The strong dominate. The weak submit. Either you fear them or they fear you. If you don't dominate others, you're one of the weak, like cattle. The only thing that matters is to win. It doesn't matter how. It doesn't matter what you do or how you talk, as long as you seem certain. Be confident, and let them project all their hopes and fears onto you, and each person will say, he's one of us. He says what I am thinking! This is how you win over the stupid. You tell them, we're going to make Italy great again! And those assholes actually believe you. It's all bullshit. WILL SOMEBODY PLEASE SHUT UP THOSE GODDAMNED OWLS?

PIRANDELLO. Are you feeling all right? You seem to be not quite yourself.

IL DUCE. The last thing a man can afford to be is himself. It's like everybody I know is a character in one of your ridiculous plays. Everything is a farce. This ship is going down, and all I have to eat is slop. Why can't I get good lasagna any more? Doesn't anybody here remember how to make lasagna? We must make lasagna great again!

(*Pause.*)

All right. Maybe I am a little tense. I know I'm supposed to be in charge here, but I'm feeling more and more like a prisoner in my own nightmare. People come by to genuflect and then piss on my shoes. I feel like there's something I should be remembering that I can't quite. Do you think I'm losing my mind? Don't answer that. Is it true your wife is insane?

PIRANDELLO. My wife is seriously ill, yes. But then, a woman is like a dream. She's never quite what you expected.

IL DUCE. Actually, most women are exactly what I expected. Does she still let you fuck her?

PIRANDELLO. I really don't feel comfortable answering questions of that nature.

IL DUCE. So the answer is no. Well, at least you've got that good looking mistress. That actress. She's quite a beauty.

PIRANDELLO. If he wishes to remain sane, a man should never love an actress. She's already twenty other people before you even know the person you thought she was when you met her. Whoever you think she is, you're wrong, and you will keep being wrong no matter what you do. A man can either accept this or shoot himself in the head. Those are basically the only two options.

IL DUCE. So you're fucking this actress.

PIRANDELLO. I really don't want to talk about this.

IL DUCE. Come on. You can tell me. It's a simple question. Are you fucking her or aren't you?

PIRANDELLO. What happened between that young woman and me – it was – everything in my life changed one night, in my hotel room, when the company was on tour.

IL DUCE. So that's when you fucked her?

> (**THE ACTRESS** *enters, much younger than* **PIRANDELLO**, *in a rather revealing nightgown. We are seeing what happened in that hotel room, or at least one possible version of it.* **IL DUCE** *remains and watches.*)

THE ACTRESS. I took a chance you might still be awake. You don't sleep much, do you? I don't, either. It's an occupational hazard of theatre people, I think. The only way we can ever calm down and focus on anything is when we're pretending to be somebody else.

PIRANDELLO. Sometimes I stay up late and write.

THE ACTRESS. I hope you don't mind me coming to your room, so late at night. I don't want to disturb you.

PIRANDELLO. No. You're very welcome, at any time. I just didn't expect you.

THE ACTRESS. The best things that happen in one's life are often the most unexpected.

PIRANDELLO. Yes. But also the worst.

(Pause.)

THE ACTRESS. So, the show is going well, don't you think?

PIRANDELLO. The show is coming along. It could be better. You are wonderful.

THE ACTRESS. I could also be better. I never quite seem to get it right. I figure out one thing and that throws everything else off. I'm never satisfied. I've always been restless. Looking for something. I don't know what. And when I can't sleep, I wander. I'm feeling very strange tonight. On edge. The moon seems larger than it was. Could it be closer to the earth? I can't help having this feeling that something is going to happen tonight. Do you ever feel that way? That immense sense of inexplicable anticipation, the irrational certainty that something is about to happen that's going to change your life forever?

PIRANDELLO. What would that be? The moon crashing into the earth?

THE ACTRESS. Or perhaps something less catastrophic. Something wonderful.

(Pause.)

How do you feel about me?

PIRANDELLO. You know how I feel about you.

THE ACTRESS. I don't, actually. You picked me out of a hundred girls to be the leading actress in your plays. You've taught me so much. Trusted me with your work. And, to be frank, you give every indication of being in love with me. But you never do anything about it. You're always such a gentleman.

PIRANDELLO. I respect you.

THE ACTRESS. Respect is good. Respect is very important. Especially in a profession in which women do not get a great deal of respect from the men they work with, or anybody else, for that matter. I sincerely appreciate the respectful way you have always treated me. I really do. And I'm immensely grateful. For everything. But, you know, respect and desire are not mutually exclusive.

PIRANDELLO. I know that. But as a married man, it's really impossible for me to act otherwise.

THE ACTRESS. That is not, in my experience, necessarily the case.

PIRANDELLO. Unfortunately, it is for me.

THE ACTRESS. So you love your wife? I only ask because you seem to be such an unhappy man.

PIRANDELLO. I will always love my wife. At least, a part of me will. But she's exhausting. She's suspicious of everything and everybody. She throws outrageous tantrums. And she's absolutely convinced that I'm betraying her with actresses, schoolgirls. Every woman I come in contact with.

THE ACTRESS. But you're not.

PIRANDELLO. No. I'm not.

THE ACTRESS. You sound as if you regret being loyal to her. You have a choice, you know. You can choose the sort of life you want. If it makes you so unhappy, and so lonely, is it really necessary to deny yourself any pleasure in life at all, just so you can be loyal to someone who makes you miserable?

PIRANDELLO. In an ideal world, it would be nice to be able to share my life with somebody who was not insane.

THE ACTRESS. And yet you've devoted yourself to the theatre, which is often controlled by the mediocre, who are mostly stupid, and a small number of people with real genius, who are mostly insane.

PIRANDELLO. It's true. I wrote my first play when I was twelve, and produced it on the landing of the steps in our garden. It was quite a scandal. It was going very well until a boy who was upset I didn't cast him jumped out from behind a pillar and urinated on the stage. It was actually the most interesting and honest part of the performance. I suspect that everything I've done in the theatre since then probably flows – so to speak – from that initial transgression. I'm drawn to the theatre because it feels like there's more truth here than any place else. The theatre is made of lies, but so is everything else. At least in the theatre we acknowledge that we're constructing an elaborate unreality in order to investigate possible realities we can't see when we're out in the world pretending we know what's real. If I must spend my life groping about in the dark, I'd rather it be in a theatre.

THE ACTRESS. Sometimes I look across the stage at you in rehearsal and I feel so bad for you. You seem like the saddest man on the face of the earth. And I have this almost overpowering urge to comfort you.

PIRANDELLO. It means a lot to me that you would feel that way.

THE ACTRESS. So, would you like me to?

PIRANDELLO. Would I like you to what?

THE ACTRESS. To comfort you. Because if you need company tonight – let me know. And I will. I'll stay with you. And comfort you.

(Pause.)

PIRANDELLO. As much as I would like that, and I really would very, very much like that, I think that, as wonderful as that would be – it might lead to a situation which, in the end, you would regret. And I would feel so terrible that you regretted it. And it could poison our relationship forever, and threaten our work together. You and I have built a good working relationship. A close working relationship. Which I treasure.

THE ACTRESS. Couldn't we just decide to keep these things separate? Our work together would be one reality, and our private relations would be another.

PIRANDELLO. The history of human relations both in and outside the theatre would strongly suggest that it's extremely unlikely we could do that.

THE ACTRESS. So in other words, you don't want me?

PIRANDELLO. It's not a question of what I want.

THE ACTRESS. Of course it's a question of what you want. Everything is a question of what a person wants. What else is there?

PIRANDELLO. I just think that you'll have a better career and a happier personal life if we don't add an extra layer of complication to our relationship.

THE ACTRESS. An extra layer of complication?

PIRANDELLO. What I mean is –

THE ACTRESS. All right. Fine. I'm sorry I bothered you.

PIRANDELLO. You didn't bother me. On the contrary, I just –

THE ACTRESS. No. It's really fine. I'll just go back to my room and work on my lines. It's no problem. God forbid that I should become an added layer of complication in your life. I'll see you in the morning.

(She goes.)

PIRANDELLO. No. Wait. I didn't mean to –

IL DUCE. And then of course you followed her to her room.

PIRANDELLO. No.

IL DUCE. You didn't follow her to her room? Because that was practically an engraved invitation to follow her back to her room, take her in your arms and make passionate love to her.

PIRANDELLO. But how could a person possibly be expected to know that?

IL DUCE. Any idiot could see that.

PIRANDELLO. I took her at her word.

IL DUCE. She didn't want you to take her at her word. She wanted you to follow her to her room and jump on her. Did you think a woman would come to your room half dressed in the middle of the night just to hear about the time the boy urinated on the stage?

PIRANDELLO. I'm not a mind reader. How can I possibly know what's going on in another person's mind? Especially a woman. It could be anything.

IL DUCE. So let me get this straight. You had this beautiful young actress in a skimpy negligee in your room late at night offering to comfort you, willing to give herself to you, so you told her a story about a boy urinating on a stage and sent her away?

PIRANDELLO. I didn't send her away. She went away.

IL DUCE. And it never occurred to you to follow her to her room and make love to her?

PIRANDELLO. Of course not. What kind of man do you think I am?

IL DUCE. Not much of one, from the evidence presented so far. You didn't find this woman attractive?

PIRANDELLO. I found her enormously attractive.

IL DUCE. But you did nothing about it.

PIRANDELLO. I couldn't betray my wife.

IL DUCE. Why the hell not?

PIRANDELLO. Because it's wrong.

IL DUCE. Are you completely insane? When you have a chance to make love to a beautiful woman you grab her and throw her down on the sofa. That's what you do. Trust me. I've always been successful with women. As a young man I used to go out in the dark and prowl the streets. When I saw one I liked, I'd follow her home, catch her on the stairs, push her in a corner and take her against the wall. Then afterwards she'd start bawling at me about how I'd stolen her honor and God knows what other rubbish. I never could understand just what kind of honor she thought she was talking about. If she had any honor, what was she doing walking the streets in the middle of the night? Women are very mysterious in their own minds, and in the minds of men they don't want. You can hide behind your noble sentiments all you like, but men and women were designed to fornicate. The man has the penis, so it's his job to stick it in there whenever he can. And if he doesn't, no matter what they say, women have absolute contempt for him. Look who's successful with women. The gentle, sensitive, understanding souls? Shit, no. People like me. I rest my case.

PIRANDELLO. One needs to respect women.

IL DUCE. How can I respect a woman if she doesn't respect me? And how can she respect me if I don't show her who's boss? The place between a woman's legs isn't there to store walnuts. For courtship, candy and flowers are fine, but brass knuckles and a knife are a much better investment. For a famous writer you seem awfully stupid about women. But everybody has his blind spot. Yours seems to be that crazy wife of yours. Why are you letting her ruin your life when there's so much low hanging fruit you could just reach out and grab any time you want?

PIRANDELLO. The truth is, I usually don't understand why I do things. I hear myself saying something and I wonder, where the hell did that come from? I make up reasons afterwards but who knows why a man does this and not that? Things are connected inside our heads in ways we don't understand. We construct traps for ourselves like the net Agamemnon died in. You fall into the web and the more you struggle the more spiders come to eat you.

IL DUCE. It was his wife who killed him, wasn't it?

PIRANDELLO. Yes. In his bath water. His death was a parody of his birth.

IL DUCE. You see what women are like? You turn your back and they cut your throat.

PIRANDELLO. She killed him because he cheated on her.

IL DUCE. Of course he cheated on her. If she didn't want a husband who cheated on her she shouldn't have gotten married in the first place. You can't still be in love with your wife. Every sane person gets over that.

PIRANDELLO. I'm a writer. I don't get over anything. My marriage was always a nightmare. My father picked my wife before I knew her. I never kissed her until the wedding ceremony. I do ask myself sometimes why I agreed to marry the first woman my father set in front of me. But a person is destined to be miserable in any case. She's my wife, and I must deal with it.

THE WIFE. *(Calling from off.)* Pirandello. Pirandello.

PIRANDELLO. I speak of her and she appears, on cue. Like the catastrophe in an old play. Although if I were writing this, her entrance would not be so –

THE WIFE. *(Entering.)* I've been looking everywhere for you. Why are you always hiding?

PIRANDELLO. I'm not hiding. I've been here writing.

THE WIFE. Writing is hiding. And I know why you're always lurking around this theatre. You've been fornicating with that slut of an actress in the prop room.

PIRANDELLO. I haven't been fornicating with anybody anywhere.

THE WIFE. Liar. Playwright. You betray me over and over again. You're insatiable. Even the schoolgirls in your classes at the women's college are all hot for you.

PIRANDELLO. That's not true. It's also not my fault.

THE WIFE. Well, which is it? Not true, or not your fault?

PIRANDELLO. Yes. And you've got to stop spying on me. How am I supposed to teach my classes when half the time you're lurking out there behind an olive tree, peeking in the window at me? If I was going to betray you, it wouldn't be with a bunch of schoolgirls.

THE WIFE. No. It would be with that actress you're always mooning at like a person with brain damage.

PIRANDELLO. If you think so little of my character, then why do you care who I sleep with?

THE WIFE. Because you're my husband.

PIRANDELLO. And I'm faithful to you. Why can't you believe that?

THE WIFE. A faithful man is like a five legged camel. You can imagine one, but you can't find one. Don't try convincing me I'm married to a five legged camel.

PIRANDELLO. I wish you were married to a camel.

THE WIFE. A camel would be a better husband. On our wedding night, you just shook hands with me, turned over and went to sleep.

IL DUCE. You shook hands and went to sleep? On your wedding night?

PIRANDELLO. This is really none of your business.

IL DUCE. What the hell kind of Italian are you? I've got to say, I'm really beginning to worry about you, pal. Maybe you don't have a dick.

PIRANDELLO. She was very young. I could see that she was terrified. I was being sensitive to her feelings.

THE WIFE. My feelings were that if your husband just wants to shake hands on your wedding night, you'd better plant some cucumbers in your garden.

PIRANDELLO. We had three children, didn't we?

THE WIFE. I had three children. You were too busy making up stories to notice.

IL DUCE. So they're not his children?

PIRANDELLO. Of course they're my children.

IL DUCE. So he does have a dick?

PIRANDELLO. Can we please stop talking about my dick?

THE WIFE. He has a dick.

IL DUCE. You've actually seen it?

THE WIFE. He has one, and he knows how to use it. The truth is, he's insatiable. He has this desperate need to copulate like dogs. In the bedroom, in the kitchen, in the bathroom, in the garden, in the tool shed, in the taxi. And if I don't happen to feel like it, he whines and pouts and feels sorry for himself. And when I let him, he pretends to feel guilty after.

PIRANDELLO. I do feel guilty. I feel enslaved by lust. It's humiliating.

THE WIFE. If you didn't want to use me like a whore you'd have let me go a long time ago. You jump on me every time I turn around. And sometimes when I don't turn around. You want to do it backwards, and sideways, and hanging upside down. You tell everybody I'm crazy, but you can't get enough of me. And then your father lost my dowry when his stinking sulphur mine flooded, and there went my life. And now you're trying to poison me.

PIRANDELLO. You know that isn't true.

THE WIFE. True? You have the gall to preach to me about what's true? You're a playwright. You lie for a living.

PIRANDELLO. I'm not trying to poison you. This is a fantasy of yours. People who are demented or in love or in the grip of some other deeply irrational passion create an alternate reality and live in it. To them, anyone who questions that reality or offers a different view of what's real is a liar. You've created a reality in which I'm unfaithful to you with a thousand women. But it's a fantasy.

IL DUCE. How exactly do you do it sideways? Or upside down? Actually, that reminds me of something. What is it? Some sort of dream in which I was a bat? Or maybe an owl. Do owls hang upside down?

THE WIFE. Even when you're not doing it, you think about it all the time.

PIRANDELLO. Only because you talk about it all the time.

THE WIFE. So you admit you think about it all the time.

PIRANDELLO. I think about a lot of things I don't do.

IL DUCE. I do everything I think about immediately. It makes life so much simpler.

THE WIFE. If I'm so horrible then why don't you just let me go?

PIRANDELLO. Because you're my wife and you're not in your right mind.

THE WIFE. If I'm insane it's because you've driven me insane. One of these days when you come home and want to copulate with me like a dog I won't be there. I'll be gone. And then what will you do? Probably copulate with the dog.

PIRANDELLO. If you run away I'll just find you and bring you home again.

THE WIFE. You just want me to stay so we can keep making each other miserable, because it excites you to have sexual intercourse with a woman who's telling you what a monster you are. You can't force me to live with you.

PIRANDELLO. You should be ashamed, making such a spectacle of yourself. What would your father say?

THE WIFE. My father never could stand you. The very idea of you soiling his daughter's precious white body always filled him with disgust and horror. All the time you were courting me, my father acted like a jealous maniac.

THE FATHER-IN-LAW. *(Entering.)* Antonietta. How could you behave in that disgraceful way?

THE WIFE. What? What did I do? I was just sitting there. I didn't say a word the whole time.

THE FATHER-IN-LAW. You looked your fiancé directly in the face. Don't try and deny it. I saw you. It was disgusting. I forbid you to look directly into that man's face until after you're married.

THE WIFE. Papa, if I can't look him in the face, where am I supposed to look? How about his elbow? Can I look at his elbow?

THE FATHER-IN-LAW. Don't look at anything.

THE WIFE. I've got to look somewhere. How about his crotch? I could look at his crotch.

THE FATHER-IN-LAW. No. You can't look at his crotch. What an idea.

THE WIFE. What do you want me to do? Walk around with my eyes closed? Wear a potato sack over my head?

THE FATHER-IN-LAW. This engagement was a terrible idea.

THE WIFE. It was your idea. You're the one who arranged it in the first place.

THE FATHER-IN-LAW. Yes, because I heard this Pirandello person was an intelligent, relatively decent young man with a bright future in the sulfur mines. But the better I get to know him, the weirder he seems. I don't trust anybody who spends so much time sitting on his backside and scribbling. What on earth is ever going to come of that? I've decided we should disengage with him and marry you to Mr Pizzerelli's grandson.

THE WIFE. I don't know Mr Pizzerelli's grandson.

THE FATHER-IN-LAW. You've seen him in church. He's a very successful manufacturer of mouse traps.

THE WIFE. The one with his hair parted in the middle who's always blowing his nose?

THE FATHER-IN-LAW. He's not always blowing his nose. Sometimes he blows his nose. Everybody blows their nose. It's not his fault. He's allergic to incense. And pork. And waffles. And I think cheese.

THE WIFE. I don't want to marry a man who manufactures mouse traps and blows his nose when he eats waffles. I want Pirandello.

THE FATHER-IN-LAW. What's wrong with manufacturing mouse traps? At least mouse traps are useful. Pirandello is suffering from the illusion that he's some sort of writer. And not even a writer. A playwright. Who could possibly imagine a more ridiculous occupation? I might just as well marry you off to a circus clown. Or the Devil.

THE WIFE. I'm not marrying a circus clown or the Devil, and I'm certainly not marrying a nose-blowing mouse trap manufacturer who's allergic to cheese.

THE FATHER-IN-LAW. The duty of a daughter is to marry her father. I mean, to obey her father. To marry the person chosen by her father. I have spoken. I won't hear anything more about it.

THE WIFE. I'm marrying Pirandello and that's all there is to it. I also have spoken. And if you don't like it, you can just go sit in the corn crib and talk to your dick.

THE FATHER-IN-LAW. Talk to my dick? Talk to my dick? What can a person do with a girl like that?

IL DUCE. I can think of a number of things.

THE FATHER-IN-LAW. I believe she's completely insane.

THE WIFE. You want me to marry the Devil and a circus clown and I'm insane?

THE FATHER-IN-LAW. I need a drink.

IL DUCE. There's a bottle with some glasses over here beside the stuffed owl. Is this any good?

PIRANDELLO. I don't know. Garibaldi's got liquor hidden all over the theatre. He says it's for the ghosts, but I think he drinks most of it. I had a sip once and it tasted like motor oil.

THE WIFE. If it's poison, I'll drink it. My marriage is a nightmare.

>   (**IL DUCE** *is pouring the wine into two glasses and giving one to* **THE FATHER-IN-LAW**.)

PIRANDELLO. You chose to marry me. Nobody forced you.

THE WIFE. You tell everybody I'm crazy, but you're the one who's insane. You've been insane all along. Never trust a playwright. He's got too many voices in his head.

PIRANDELLO. Well, I married you. Maybe I am insane.

THE WIFE. And much worse, you're complicit.

PIRANDELLO. Complicit in what?

THE WIFE. *(Pointing to* **IL DUCE.***)* You're complicit in the evil perpetrated by that horrible man.

IL DUCE. I'm not horrible. I'm just misunderstood.

PIRANDELLO. I'm not complicit in anything. All I do is write plays.

IL DUCE. Well, I'm a little horrible, but I'm a necessary monster, like God. If I did not exist, somebody would have to invent me.

(Takes a sip of the wine.)

This tastes like strawberries and urine.

THE FATHER-IN-LAW. *(Also sampling the wine.)* With just a hint of donkey sweat.

IL DUCE. Yes. Would you like some more?

THE FATHER-IN-LAW. Absolutely.

*(***IL DUCE** *pours more wine.)*

THE WIFE. You're a fascist.

PIRANDELLO. A lot of people are fascists.

THE WIFE. A lot of people are murderers, too. Is that an excuse?

IL DUCE. She makes a good point.

PIRANDELLO. I'm not a murderer.

THE WIFE. Everybody who supports that man is a murderer. Anybody who praises him and his psychopathic little friend Adolf has blood on their hands.

THE FATHER-IN-LAW. Adolf who? Who are you talking about? What year is this? Am I dead yet? Because I seem to remember attending my funeral. What the hell is in this wine?

THE WIFE. I don't know what year it is. Time is all confused in my head. But every night in my dreams I see piles and piles of the dead these people have murdered. And now you're trying to poison me so you can marry your whore.

PIRANDELLO. Nobody is trying to poison you.

THE WIFE. You gave me a glass of wine and I gave some to the dog, and the next day the dog died.

> (**IL DUCE** and **THE FATHER-IN-LAW** *both spit out the wine, a rather spectacular double spit-take.*)

PIRANDELLO. That dog was older than your grandmother. And he smelled better. And the dog only bit me once. Your grandmother bit me every Sunday when she got home from church.

THE FATHER-IN-LAW. It's true. We found her false teeth stuck in his pants.

THE WIFE. You think because I'm a woman you can look down your nose at me and insult my grandmother and call me crazy and get away with anything because nothing is real and nobody can know anything for certain. Well, maybe I'm crazy, but one thing I'm certain of is that my husband is a gigantic pile of hypocritical fascist bullshit.

PIRANDELLO. I've told you not to use that sort of language. What if the children should hear?

THE WIFE. Don't talk to me about the children. The children know what you are. You are a bird who has fouled his own nest.

PIRANDELLO. I don't know what you're talking about.

THE WIFE. You know exactly what I'm talking about.

PIRANDELLO. I really haven't got a clue.

THE WIFE. You know what you've done. You've violated your own daughter.

PIRANDELLO. That's disgusting.

THE WIFE. Yes it is. Look at this man. The celebrated author. And inside him is nothing but rot. This is a man who sleeps with his own daughter.

PIRANDELLO. I'm not sleeping with my daughter. I'm not sleeping with anybody. I'm not sleeping at all.

THE WIFE. Lies. You cover yourself with lies like a pig in slop. But I know the truth. I know it. You know what you did.

PIRANDELLO. Why do you say these monstrous things?

THE WIFE. Because somebody here must speak the truth.

IL DUCE. Even I wouldn't do that. And there's very little I wouldn't do.

PIRANDELLO. I never did anything of the sort. Can't you see she's totally demented?

THE WIFE. I can't allow this to go on. She can't stay in our home any longer. Our daughter must be sent away from you for good.

PIRANDELLO. Nobody is sending our daughter away.

THE WIFE. I'm not letting you touch her, ever again. She'll be far, far, far away from you.

PIRANDELLO. Where are you planning on sending her? Mars? Because if she's going to Mars, I think you should go along.

THE WIFE. Brazil. She's going to Brazil, where you can never get your hands on her again.

PIRANDELLO. Our daughter is not going to Brazil.

THE WIFE. She's going to Brazil. I'm sending her to Brazil. I've already bought the ticket.

PIRANDELLO. What the hell is our daughter going to do in Brazil?

THE WIFE. Whatever she wants, as long as you can't get your hands on her again.

IL DUCE. She might like it. They have very large nuts in Brazil.

PIRANDELLO. There is no way I will ever allow you to send our daughter to Brazil.

THE WIFE. Can't you do at least one decent thing in your life and let her go? Isn't it enough that she's already tried to poison herself?

PIRANDELLO. She tried to poison herself because she couldn't stand listening to the horrible things you were saying about us.

THE WIFE. Liar. You blame me for everything because you can't face the truth. I can't stand this. FIEND. MONSTER. PLAYWRIGHT.

(**THE WIFE** *goes off.*)

THE FATHER-IN-LAW. There. See what you've done? Now she'll break all that's left of my mother's good china and push the piano off the balcony again. I wish I'd never had children. I should have just gotten a turtle.

IL DUCE. I like her. She's crazy as a bag of rats, but surprisingly attractive. I've always liked them a little bit out of their minds. It adds a kind of frenzy to the sex. Don't you find that?

THE FATHER-IN-LAW. Her mother was insane, too. One day I came home and she'd eaten the parrot. And that parrot was the only person in the house I actually enjoyed talking to.

PIRANDELLO. You mustn't pay any attention to anything she says. My wife is very ill. And very unhappy.

IL DUCE. Yes, well, who isn't? So, are you?

PIRANDELLO. Am I what?

IL DUCE. Sleeping with your daughter?

PIRANDELLO. Of course not.

IL DUCE. It's all right. You can tell me.

PIRANDELLO. I have never slept with my daughter.

IL DUCE. But didn't you write a play about a man who wanted to sleep with his daughter? The one with the six characters searching for an author, or a plot, or something like that?

THE FATHER-IN-LAW. You see? He's a pervert. I knew it. Playwrights are not entirely human.

(Sound of dishes breaking, off.)

There goes my Grandmother's soup tureen. Well, the cat used to pee in it, anyway.

PIRANDELLO. In the play it was his step-daughter. And he only thought about sleeping with her because he didn't recognize her at the brothel.

IL DUCE. A small conjuring trick designed by the author to disguise his forbidden desire.

PIRANDELLO. No. That's absolutely revolting.

IL DUCE. What's revolting for some is exciting for others. But, as I heard a wise man say once, not long ago, in fact, on this very stage, what is truth? How can we be certain of anything? Especially when it comes to human behavior. It's all right. Everybody's a monster in the dark.

PIRANDELLO. It's not all right. Now she's going to have everybody believing it. People are so ready to see filth. When I was a boy, on a dare, I snuck into the morgue in the tower to see a corpse. I was staring in horror at the poor dead thing before me when I heard something which sounded like animal noises and saw that there in the shadows, not far from the corpse, a man and a woman were copulating ferociously against a wall. The realities of love and death have been hopelessly mixed in my head ever since. Why is love constantly being poisoned by miscomprehension, stained by madness, and destroyed by betrayal? It's enough to drive a person to despair.

THE FATHER-IN-LAW. If you've been molesting my granddaughter, I'm afraid I have no choice but to challenge you to a duel.

PIRANDELLO. I haven't been molesting anybody, and I'm not fighting a duel.

THE FATHER-IN-LAW. As the challenged party, of course, you get to choose weapons.

IL DUCE. Pick salad forks. I've always felt that salad forks were underrated for dueling. Salad forks make it much more personal, don't you think?

THE FATHER-IN-LAW. Salad forks. Well, maybe there's some here under all this rubbish.

(He begins rummaging around in the scattered props.)

PIRANDELLO. When did my life begin to turn into this grotesque farce? There's a tempest in my head all the time now.

IL DUCE. Well, before your father-in-law disembowels you with a salad fork, I just want to reaffirm that I remain a great admirer of your work, and really appreciate you helping me confirm what I've always suspected – that you can make anything seem real to people if you just keep repeating it over and over again.

PIRANDELLO. But that's not what I meant to suggest. What I meant was –

IL DUCE. Shut up. I'm teaching you something about what you taught me. You said it yourself, in that play about the man who was pretending to be pretending he was pretending to be somebody he actually was.

PIRANDELLO. *Henry IV*?

IL DUCE. I don't know. All your plays are like that. The point is, he says if you can't pretend, you can't be king. And it's true. The state is an elaborate fiction, like money, or God. Government is a fiction, like love, or honesty. And I, Il Duce, am the supreme fiction – the greatest imaginary personage since Pinocchio. And according to you, if one chooses to believe, say, that Hitler's extermination camps aren't real, then poof, like magic, they vanish. It's wonderful.

PIRANDELLO. I don't know anything about extermination camps. All I was trying to get at was, what can we really know for certain about what other people take to be reality? The reason life keeps reducing itself to a sort of sad clown show is that we all have lurking within us the need to constantly be deceiving ourselves by creating around us a reality which we keep discovering again and again is a vain illusion.

IL DUCE. In other words, whatever I say, that's the truth.

PIRANDELLO. I didn't say that. Did I say that? God, maybe I did say that. When I was a child, I thought the moon's reflection in a pond was real. But when you reach for it, there's nothing there. The night I was born there were thousands of fireflies, and everybody thought it was a sign of some sort, but nobody could agree on what, because although everything is a symbol, it's not the same symbol for everybody. It's dangerous to write anything, because no matter what you say, everything is misunderstood and used to prove things you didn't intend. I don't know what's real. Nobody knows what's real. We don't even know what real means.

THE FATHER-IN-LAW. I can't find any salad forks, but here's a box of dueling pistols. What about these? I should warn you, I once killed a man with a dueling pistol. We kept missing each other until we ran out of ammunition so I finally just whacked him over the head with it until he stopped moving.

PIRANDELLO. Marionettes. Everything is marionettes. In the shop where they sold the marionettes, when I was a child, that was heaven. If I could only be there again.

IL DUCE. Sex is real.

THE FATHER-IN-LAW. But only while it's happening.

PIRANDELLO. No. Sex seems the most unreal of all while one is doing it. But just to hold someone in one's arms, to feel her heart beating and know you're loved –

IL DUCE. Yes, but then the husband comes home and you've got to climb out the window.

THE FATHER-IN-LAW. Does that happen to you, too? I've still got scars on my butt from Mrs Tagliotti's rose bush.

IL DUCE. It used to happen to me all the time. Now I just send the husbands to the Russian front. It saves time.

PIRANDELLO. I'm not talking about the sort of sordid comedy where you end up climbing out the window. There is such a thing as love. There is. It's just that whoever is writing the play keeps putting it off to the next act.

IL DUCE. So if nobody knows what's real, then maybe you slept with your daughter.

PIRANDELLO. I did not sleep with my daughter.

IL DUCE. How do you know if nobody knows what's real?

THE ACTRESS. *(Returning, this time dressed.)* When I saw the light, I knew it was you. What are you doing still at the theatre so late at night?

PIRANDELLO. I don't know. Talking to people who aren't here.

THE ACTRESS. I'm here.

PIRANDELLO. Are you sure?

THE ACTRESS. Pretty sure.

PIRANDELLO. What are you doing here?

THE ACTRESS. You know I can't sleep. I get restless and go out walking, and I always end up here. The theatre is the only place that feels real to me. There's a lot of fog out there tonight. You can't even see the street signs. It's easy to get lost.

PIRANDELLO. Yes.

THE ACTRESS. You're not looking well. You should go home and get some rest.

PIRANDELLO. I will if you'll come with me.

THE ACTRESS. We've been through that a long time ago.

PIRANDELLO. I know, but I'm feeling very strange tonight. Strange things are happening in my head. I just need to hold you.

THE ACTRESS. That's what they all say.

PIRANDELLO. So now you don't trust me?

THE ACTRESS. How can I trust a man who doesn't believe I'm real?

PIRANDELLO. I believe you're real.

THE ACTRESS. You don't believe anybody is real.

PIRANDELLO. I don't know what I believe. You can't imagine how tired and lonely I feel at this moment. I need you.

THE ACTRESS. Don't tell me that. You had your chance. I offered myself up to you completely that night in the hotel. And what did you do? Did you embrace me? Did you make love to me? No. You were rational. You were sensible. You gave me a lecture about why a woman of my age shouldn't waste herself on a man as old as you, and why it would be bad for our working relationship if we were lovers. What a load of crap that was.

PIRANDELLO. It was all the truth.

THE ACTRESS. I don't care if it was the truth. It was humiliating. Can you possibly imagine how incredibly insulting it was for a woman like me to offer herself up completely to a man like you and be rejected so brutally?

PIRANDELLO. You caught me off guard. I hardly knew what I was saying. I was trying to do the right thing.

THE ACTRESS. And who exactly was it supposed to be the right thing for? The lonely old man who had a chance at some intimate human contact and threw it away, or the young woman who humiliated herself and sat waiting for him in her room all night?

PIRANDELLO. The right thing for both of us. The right thing in the eyes of a God I don't actually believe in but whose somewhat confused precepts about how to behave I still have a certain amount of respect for, despite everything. And I didn't want to take advantage of you.

THE ACTRESS. What a patronizing thing to say.

PIRANDELLO. And I was afraid.

THE ACTRESS. Afraid of what? Of me?

PIRANDELLO. No. Not of you. Well, yes, of you. Of allowing myself to unleash feelings for you that I knew you couldn't sustain for me. I was afraid of the look I'd see on your face when you realized you'd made a terrible mistake. Of the look of pity when you saw me, finally, as just a pathetic, infatuated old man.

THE ACTRESS. Everybody who loves takes the risk of being made to look ridiculous. Either you have the courage to love or you don't.

PIRANDELLO. You really waited for me all night?

THE ACTRESS. It doesn't matter now.

PIRANDELLO. I've rehearsed that night over and over again a thousand times. I think about you all the time. I write to keep from going mad. I dream about you. Sometimes in my dreams you love me. I go to your room and hold you in my arms and I'm so happy. But then I wake up and you're not there and I can't stop sobbing like a child. But in most of my dreams you're looking at me, in a doorway, as if you're deciding whether to come to me, to give yourself to me, or to go. And you start to come to me. But then you hear something, over your shoulder, behind you, a voice from another room, and you turn your back on me and close the door, and I want to go after you, but I can't move. Or I'm in the theatre. I'm watching a performance, from backstage. And you're there, on stage, looking so beautiful. And I want to go onstage and rescue you from the audience, because I know they can't be trusted and will hurt you, turn on you, eventually, inevitably, because an audience is a mob without a soul. But someone is holding me back. I don't know if it's my father, or Mussolini, or who it is, but they're telling me, don't go out there. Nothing is real out there. Nothing is real. And then I'm back in that hotel room, and it's the middle of the night, and the solitude is horrible, and I know that I'm alone, and I'll always be alone, I'll die alone, and I'll never see you again. Why must reality be only one thing? I want the reality in which I never let you leave that room. And now you continue to punish me over and over again for the terrible sin of trying to behave like a decent person.

THE ACTRESS. What happens between men and women has very little to do with decency.

IL DUCE. You see? She agrees with me. What did I tell you?

THE ACTRESS. *(Turning around, startled to see* **IL DUCE** *and* **THE FATHER-IN-LAW** *watching them.)* What the hell are they doing here?

PIRANDELLO. I don't know. I'm not even sure they're actually here. I'm not even sure I'm here.

IL DUCE. Listen, my poor, confused friend. I don't mean to intrude, but, really, you're going about this all wrong.

PIRANDELLO. Just stay out of this. This is none of your concern.

IL DUCE. But no woman who was ever born on the face of the earth could possibly love a man who behaves like you. First you reject and humiliate her and then you beg her. You might get her to pity you, acting like that, but not enough to sleep with you. She's going to continue to torture you as long as you let her, but she'll sleep with somebody with balls.

THE ACTRESS. Just what do you know about it?

IL DUCE. I know that nobody wants desperation. Admit it. You like the feeling of having power over him.

THE ACTRESS. Well, you know something about getting excited by power, don't you?

IL DUCE. Exactly. Power is better than sex, because if you have power, you can get all the sex you want, because, really, who's going to stop you? But to watch this poor jackass humiliating himself over and over again, it must sicken you even while it excites you.

PIRANDELLO. You're right, of course. When an old man loves a young woman, he deserves all the humiliation he gets. But I can't seem to help it. It's like I've been cast in a role and I can't get out of it. Sometimes I feel so much love it just overwhelms me. I can't think straight, and I can't seem to control what I say or do. Things just fly out of my mouth like bats out of a cave. I feel too much.

IL DUCE. It's not that you feel too much, it's that what you're feeling is bullshit. Romantic love is an illusion, like a stage play. It can be quite entertaining while you're experiencing it. But it doesn't last long. And what sane person would want it to? Sooner or later the play ends, and you go out into the night and grope around in the fog until you stumble into another reality, where you can find another deluded person to pretend you're in love with.

THE ACTRESS. This is not a play.

IL DUCE. Well, not much of one, but don't blame Pirandello. One's powers inevitably fail in old age. Except for mine, of course. I'm regularly injected with pig semen.

THE FATHER-IN-LAW. Does that work?

IL DUCE. Surprisingly enough, yes. The only drawback is that pigs follow you around in the street. In any case, my dear, if you don't want him, I'm available. And lucky for you, I have no scruples whatsoever.

THE FATHER-IN-LAW. *(Holding the box of pistols up in front of PIRANDELLO.)* So. Which pistol do you want?

PIRANDELLO. I'm not fighting a duel with you. Dueling is stupid.

THE FATHER-IN-LAW. Of course it's stupid. Most of our male rituals are stupid. But we were born slaves to our penis, so what choice do we have?

THE ACTRESS. Why does he want to fight a duel with you? And who is he? And why is he here?

PIRANDELLO. He's my father-in-law. It's just a little misunderstanding.

THE ACTRESS. I thought your father-in-law was dead.

PIRANDELLO. So did I. Time is very strange in this place. Of course, time is strange everywhere. I don't even know what time is.

IL DUCE. Time is what keeps everything from happening at once. Who said that? Did I say that? And what does it mean?

THE ACTRESS. Why is your dead father-in-law here in the theatre in the middle of the night with Mussolini?

IL DUCE. He's upset that Pirandello is sleeping with his daughter.

THE ACTRESS. But if he's your father-in-law, his daughter is your wife. Why would your father-in-law be upset that you're sleeping with your wife? And if you're sleeping with your wife, why do you need me?

IL DUCE. No. He thinks Pirandello is sleeping with his own daughter.

THE ACTRESS. You're sleeping with your daughter?

PIRANDELLO. I am not sleeping with my daughter. I am NOT sleeping with my daughter.

IL DUCE. He sounds like a man who's sleeping with his daughter.

THE FATHER-IN-LAW. He really does.

THE ACTRESS. So that's why you didn't want to sleep with me? Because you were sleeping with your daughter?

PIRANDELLO. No.

THE ACTRESS. That night in the hotel, was she hiding under your bed?

PIRANDELLO. Nobody was hiding under the bed, and nobody was sleeping with my daughter. Now, I don't want to hear anything more about it. The way this play is going, if people keep mentioning her, she's going to show up.

THE ACTRESS. Why would mentioning her make her show up?

IL DUCE. Apparently this is what happens in plays.

THE ACTRESS. No it isn't.

THE DAUGHTER. *(Entering.)* Papa, what's all this shouting going on in the theatre? I could hear it all the way down the street.

PIRANDELLO. There. You see what you've done? Who is writing this? God must be drunk.

THE DAUGHTER. What have you been saying to Mama? She's very upset.

PIRANDELLO. Your mother is always upset.

THE DAUGHTER. Yes, but this is worse. I'm very worried about her.

IL DUCE. Ah. So this is the Daughter. How wonderful to meet you, my dear. Nice. Very nice. Very, very nice.

THE DAUGHTER. What are all these people doing here? Is that Grandfather? I thought he was dead.

THE FATHER-IN-LAW. Everybody's been telling me that. It's quite possible that I am dead. I'd probably be a lot happier if I was dead.

THE DAUGHTER. And that's that actress. The one Mama – is always talking about. And what's Mussolini doing here?

PIRANDELLO. Just go back to your Mother and try to keep her calm. I'll be there in a moment.

IL DUCE. *(Putting his arm around* **THE DAUGHTER** *and pulling her downstage.)* No, no, wait, my dear. Don't be so quick to run away. You just got here, and I'd like to get to know you a little better. And also, this is our chance to settle this very interesting question once and for all.

THE DAUGHTER. What question?

PIRANDELLO. My daughter really needs to go now. Her mother mustn't be left alone.

IL DUCE. Did your mother give you any hints as to just what she's so upset about?

THE DAUGHTER. I don't know. It's difficult to understand sometimes what she's talking about. She jumps from one thing to the next, like a rabbit in a brush fire.

PIRANDELLO. Please. Just let her go back and –

IL DUCE. Just keep your pants on, Luigi. And, ironically, that's actually what this is all about.

THE DAUGHTER. I don't understand.

IL DUCE. The question here is whether or not your father was able to keep his pants on.

THE DAUGHTER. His pants? What about my father's pants?

PIRANDELLO. I really must object.

THE ACTRESS. No, no. I want to hear this.

THE DAUGHTER. Papa, why is he talking about your pants?

IL DUCE. So, tell me, my dear, is it true that you and your father –

PIRANDELLO. That's enough.

IL DUCE. That is to say, that your father and you –

PIRANDELLO. Stop this. I didn't write this. This is not part of the play.

IL DUCE. That your father ever dealt with you in a way which was – let us call it, in place of a more vulgar description – inappropriate?

THE DAUGHTER. I don't know what you mean.

IL DUCE. I understand you tried to poison yourself over it.

PIRANDELLO. For God's sake let the poor girl alone.

IL DUCE. *(Abandoning the charm for a moment, pointing at* **PIRANDELLO**, *fierce and scary.)* You stay over there. I am talking here. I am Il Duce. You are just some playwright, a very minor and highly expendable sort of a tin whistle god, and that gives you the delusion that you're important, but we both know you're no better than the rest of these weasels. You praise me to my face and make fun of me behind my back. You take the honors and privileges I bestow upon you with one hand and make obscene gestures at me with the other.

So if you don't want your daughter written out of this play permanently, just stand over there and keep your mouth shut. Are we clear? Good.

THE DAUGHTER. This is all very strange. I don't understand what's happening here.

IL DUCE. *(Leading her over to a chair and sitting down.)* Don't worry about it, sweetheart. There's nothing to be concerned about. You're perfectly safe with Old Uncle Benito. Just come and sit on my knee.

THE DAUGHTER. I don't want to sit on your knee.

IL DUCE. *(Patting his knee.)* It's all right. Come and sit. Girls sit on my knee all the time, and very little harm comes to them, mostly.

THE DAUGHTER. I really think I'd rather –

IL DUCE. SIT. NOW.

(She sits on his knee.)

Good girl. Now. Just tell us please why it was that you decided to poison yourself.

THE DAUGHTER. Papa. I can't believe you told him that.

PIRANDELLO. I didn't tell him that. Your mother did.

THE DAUGHTER. Why do you always blame everything on Mother?

IL DUCE. Yes. Why do you always blame everything on her Mother? She's the daughter. That's her job. Now, my dear, just tell us why you tried to kill yourself.

THE DAUGHTER. This is very personal.

IL DUCE. It's all right. You can tell me. I am Il Duce. The father of his people. Surely your Papa has told you many wonderful things about me. He's a great admirer of mine. If you can't trust Il Duce, who can you trust? Just tell us why a lovely young girl like you, with everything to live for, would want to put an end to her life.

THE DAUGHTER. I'm not sure. I just had this feeling come over me that I didn't want to live any more.

IL DUCE. But why wouldn't you want to live?

THE DAUGHTER. I was upset about my mother.

IL DUCE. What about your mother?

THE DAUGHTER. About her madness. And about some of the things she said. Because of her madness.

IL DUCE. And what was it your mother said that upset you so much?

THE DAUGHTER. I don't want to repeat it.

IL DUCE. Well, this terrible thing that your mother said, that caused you to not want to live any more, was it true?

THE DAUGHTER. My mother said many terrible things in her madness. Some of them were true, but most of them were half truths or complete fantasies.

IL DUCE. But what about the thing that made you want to take your life? Was that a truth, a half truth, or a fantasy?

THE DAUGHTER. I think it was just her illness.

IL DUCE. You think?

THE DAUGHTER. I think so. Yes.

IL DUCE. But you're not sure? Is it difficult to tell the difference? I mean, between a truth, a half truth, and a fantasy?

THE DAUGHTER. I don't know. I don't want to talk about this.

PIRANDELLO. That's enough. Let her go.

IL DUCE. She doesn't want me to let her go. She likes it here on my lap. It's just like Papa's lap, isn't it? Now, just tell the truth. What really happened between you and your Papa?

THE DAUGHTER. What happened?

IL DUCE. Yes. Just tell us what really happened.

THE MISTRESS. *(Bursting in.)* Benito. What are you doing with that girl? GET OFF HIS LAP, YOU FILTHY LITTLE SLUT.

THE DAUGHTER. *(Jumping off* IL DUCE*'s lap.)* I'm not a slut.

THE MISTRESS. You just keep your mouth shut, whore.

THE DAUGHTER. Papa, why is this woman calling me names? I don't know what's happening here. Could somebody please tell me what's happening here?

THE MISTRESS. I leave you alone for five minutes and you find some little prostitute to sit on your lap.

THE DAUGHTER. I'm sorry, Mrs Mussolini. It was completely innocent, I promise you.

THE MISTRESS. I'm not Mrs Mussolini. I should be Mrs Mussolini but he refuses to get a divorce.

IL DUCE. What can I do? The Pope won't let me.

THE MISTRESS. You're not married to the Pope. You don't give a shit about the Pope.

IL DUCE. Clara, she's telling the truth. It was completely innocent.

THE DAUGHTER. Papa, what is happening? Why are these people here? Why is he asking me all these questions?

PIRANDELLO. *(Coming over and putting his hands on her shoulders.)* It's all right. Everything is all right.

THE DAUGHTER. *(Moving uneasily away from* PIRANDELLO.*)* Please don't touch me.

PIRANDELLO. I'm your father. I just want to comfort you. What's wrong?

THE DAUGHTER. I just don't want anybody touching me right now. I'm confused.

PIRANDELLO. Confused about what?

THE DAUGHTER. Everything. Nothing seems real.

PIRANDELLO. *(Holding her.)* I'm your father and I love you. That's real.

THE WIFE. *(Running in and pulling* **PIRANDELLO** *away from* **THE DAUGHTER.***)* You. Get your filthy hands off her, you demon come from Hell. In front of all these people, even. Have you no shame?

PIRANDELLO. I'm comforting my daughter.

THE WIFE. Yes, we know how you comfort your daughter.

THE FATHER-IN-LAW. It's all right. I'm going to shoot him.

IL DUCE. Wait until he finishes my play. Then you can shoot him.

THE DAUGHTER. This is like a nightmare. Is this a nightmare?

THE ACTRESS. It's a theatre. The theatre is quite often a nightmare.

THE WIFE. Every theatre is a brothel and everyone who works there is a prostitute.

(Pointing to **THE ACTRESS.***)*

Like you.

(Noticing **THE MISTRESS.***)*

And there's another one. Planning an orgy, are you?

THE MISTRESS. I beg your pardon.

THE FATHER-IN-LAW. She's not your husband's whore. She's Il Duce's whore.

THE MISTRESS. Benito, are you going to let him talk about me that way?

IL DUCE. Well, I could kill him, but his granddaughter says he's already dead, so what would be the point?

THE MISTRESS. How could he be dead? He doesn't look dead. Well, not very dead. Is she crazy?

IL DUCE. I don't know. She tried to kill herself, so she must be seeing things pretty clearly. Her mother is crazy.

THE WIFE. I'm not crazy. My husband is crazy. He thinks he can play with us all, as if we were the puppets he spent all his time jabbering with when he was a child. And he's got his own child so confused she doesn't know what she's doing. Do you see what you've done to her? She's a terrible mess. She eats like a pig, throws up everything, then won't eat for days. She goes to stores and buys everything in sight. Our house is full of ceramic pigs. What am I supposed to do with four hundred ceramic pigs? Every time I turn around I knock over a pig.

THE DAUGHTER. There's nothing wrong with ceramic pigs. I like pigs. At least I like them better than people. And spending money keeps me from thinking. Thinking is very painful. It hurts my head. I don't ever want to think about anything again. There's too much in my head already.

THE WIFE. It's all your father's fault. He believes we're all just characters in one of his stupid plays, and he can do whatever he pleases with us, and spend all his time running after all these whores.

THE MISTRESS. Who is this person who keeps calling everybody a whore?

THE WIFE. I'm his wife.

THE MISTRESS. You're not Benito's wife. Benito's wife has a mustache.

IL DUCE. My wife doesn't have a mustache.

THE MISTRESS. Then why do you have all that mustache wax?

IL DUCE. To put on my mustache.

THE MISTRESS. But you don't have a mustache.

IL DUCE. Yes, but they were having a sale. You never know when you're going to run out of mustache wax.

THE MISTRESS. How can you run out of mustache wax if you don't have a mustache?

IL DUCE. I don't know. Maybe the mice are eating it.

THE MISTRESS. How many mice do you know who eat mustache wax?

THE WIFE. I'm Pirandello's wife. My husband has a mustache. But oddly enough, we have no mustache wax.

THE MISTRESS. If you're his wife, then what was he doing with his hands all over her?

PIRANDELLO. My hands weren't all over anybody. I was just trying to comfort my daughter. A father can comfort his daughter.

THE FATHER-IN-LAW. If you try comforting her again, I'm going to shoot off your nut sack.

THE MISTRESS. If she's not a whore, then what was she doing on your lap?

IL DUCE. She was sad. She's Pirandello's daughter. Wouldn't you be sad if you were Pirandello's daughter?

THE MISTRESS. So it's all right for her to sit on your lap because she's Pirandello's daughter? Can anybody follow that logic? You know how much I love you, and yet you treat me like some sort of common dance hall floozy.

IL DUCE. You are not a common floozy. You are very uncommon.

THE WIFE. *(Pointing to* **THE ACTRESS.***)* If this isn't a brothel then what is that woman doing here?

PIRANDELLO. She's an actress. It's a theatre. She works here.

THE WIFE. At four o'clock in the morning?

THE MISTRESS. You are the love of my life. I would do anything for you. I would die for you.

IL DUCE. All right. Good to know.

THE MISTRESS. What do you mean, all right, good to know? You want me to die?

IL DUCE. At this point I'd be grateful if you'd just shut up for a while.

THE MISTRESS. How can you speak to me that way? I'm not just one of your trollops. I'm a respectable woman.

IL DUCE. Half your family are criminals, and you're sleeping with a married man.

THE MISTRESS. I'm sleeping with YOU. You're sleeping with a married woman.

IL DUCE. That's different. You're separated.

THE MISTRESS. Only because you sent my husband to Japan.

IL DUCE. Well, if you miss him, you can go to Japan, too. How did you find me here, anyway?

THE MISTRESS. I just followed the sound of the owls.

IL DUCE. You can hear the owls, too?

THE MISTRESS. Of course I can hear owls. Every time I'm with you, I hear owls. So I just followed the sound of the owls, and it led me to this theatre.

THE DAUGHTER. What owls? Why are we talking about owls? Is everybody here crazy?

THE FATHER-IN-LAW. I'm not crazy. I'm just here to kill your father for sleeping with you. But since we have no salad forks, I'll have to use a gun.

THE ACTRESS. You didn't really sleep with your daughter, did you?

PIRANDELLO. Of course not.

THE WIFE. How can you stand there and lie about it, right in front of the poor girl?

THE DAUGHTER. Mother, will you just shut up?

THE WIFE. Don't tell me to shut up. Do you want to break your mother's heart? I'm trying to send you to a nut farm in Brazil, and this is the thanks I get?

THE FATHER-IN-LAW. That's an interesting thing about the owls, though. I was actually urinated upon by an owl as I was coming in. At least, I think it was an owl. It might have been a pigeon. I don't think it was a squirrel.

THE ACTRESS. It might have been Garibaldi. He sometimes goes up on the roof to relieve himself.

THE MISTRESS. Garibaldi peed on him? I thought Garibaldi was dead.

IL DUCE. This is a different Garibaldi. It's the Father-In-Law who's dead. Try and pay attention.

THE DAUGHTER. And what is Grandfather doing here if he's dead?

THE FATHER-IN-LAW. I'm here to defend your honor.

THE DAUGHTER. I don't need anybody to defend my honor.

THE FATHER-IN-LAW. Well, if you won't, somebody's got to.

THE DAUGHTER. Just what is that supposed to mean?

THE FATHER-IN-LAW. Only that it seems quite possible to me that if your father did anything to you, you probably led him on.

THE DAUGHTER. Led him on? Led him on?

THE WIFE. *(To* **THE FATHER-IN-LAW.***)* Don't you dare speak to her that way, you hypocrite. You're as bad as he is, and you know it.

THE FATHER-IN-LAW. How can you call me a hypocrite? Here I am, ready to take a salad fork in the eye socket to defend your daughter's somewhat dubious honor, when I'm already exhausted from being dead, and you call me a hypocrite?

THE WIFE. Do you think stabbing my husband with a salad fork can ever make up for what you did to me?

THE FATHER-IN-LAW. I don't know what you mean.

THE WIFE. You know what I mean. You had your way with me when I was hardly more than a child. And now my husband has done the same thing to my daughter.

THE FATHER-IN-LAW. That's outrageous. I never did anything to you. I seldom even looked at you.

THE WIFE. Liar. All men are liars, criminals and monsters.

IL DUCE. Monster is a relative term. To a worm, a bird is a monster. To a bird, a cat is a monster. To a cat, a wolf is a monster. To a wolf, a man is a monster. To a man, God is a monster. And to God, a worm is a monster, because worms have been eating his brain ever since he died. It's the circle of life. But compared to the men in this family, I'm a better person than I thought.

THE FATHER-IN-LAW. I swear. I never did anything to her.

PIRANDELLO. You slept with your daughter, and you want to shoot me for sleeping with mine?

THE FATHER-IN-LAW. Only because I couldn't find a salad fork.

THE DAUGHTER. Stop it. Stop it, all of you. This conversation is ugly and horrible and you're all just confusing me more and more. I can't deal with this. I'm going to Brazil.

PIRANDELLO. You're not going to Brazil.

THE DAUGHTER. I am. I've got a ticket and I'm going, and you can't stop me.

PIRANDELLO. Why would you want to go to Brazil?

THE DAUGHTER. My husband is from Brazil.

PIRANDELLO. You don't have a husband.

THE DAUGHTER. I believe I have a husband. Therefore, I have a husband. It is so if I think it's so. Isn't that what you said in your play?

PIRANDELLO. But how can you have a husband I didn't know about? I've never seen your husband.

THE DAUGHTER. I've never seen Brazil, either but I know it's there. I believe Brazil is there, therefore, Brazil is there.

THE FATHER-IN-LAW. Does your husband have a nut farm? How big are his nuts?

THE DAUGHTER. Unless all of this is just some sort of dream. Is this a dream?

THE MISTRESS. I've just remembered the oddest dream.

IL DUCE. Don't tell us.

THE MISTRESS. But it was so vivid.

IL DUCE. Nobody wants to hear your dream. Nobody wants to hear anybody's dream. Unless of course there's a lot of sex in it.

THE MISTRESS. There was sex in it. And something about Pirandello.

IL DUCE. You dreamed you had sex with Pirandello?

THE MISTRESS. No. But it was so real. You and I were just about to have sex when some men entered the room.

THE FATHER-IN-LAW. Go on.

THE MISTRESS. They were dirty and bearded and had guns. We'd been running from them, but they captured us, and then they caught us, and they took you outside, and I realized they were going to shoot you, so, in my dream, I broke away from the men and ran to you, and said if they were going to shoot you, they'd have to shoot me, too.

IL DUCE. That wasn't very bright of you.

THE MISTRESS. I thought it was. Because I knew they'd never shoot a woman.

IL DUCE. So they let me go?

THE MISTRESS. No. They shot us both.

IL DUCE. And then we had sex?

THE MISTRESS. No. Then we were dead. And they hung us upside down for everyone to spit on.

IL DUCE. I told you not to eat sausages before you go to bed. It's the revenge of the pigs.

THE MISTRESS. But the strangest thing was, before you died, we were lying there in a pool of blood, it was horrible, but you looked at me, and seemed to be trying to say something, and I thought you were going to tell me that you loved me, before you died, but instead you just said one word.

IL DUCE. Shit? Was it shit?

THE MISTRESS. Pirandello.

IL DUCE. What about him? Was he upside down, too?

THE MISTRESS. No. That's the word you said. Before you died. In my dream. You said Pirandello.

IL DUCE. I said Pirandello? Why would I say Pirandello?

THE MISTRESS. How should I know? You said Pirandello. And then you died. And then I died. And then they hung us upside down.

IL DUCE. How did you know they hung us upside down if you were dead?

THE MISTRESS. It was a dream. But it was also like a play. My life was like a dream in which I was watching myself in a play. It's difficult to explain. But the last thing I heard, before I died, was the sound of rushing water, and owls.

PIRANDELLO. Owl Creek Bridge.

IL DUCE. What?

PIRANDELLO. Ambrose Bierce. A rather crabby and strange American writer. He wrote a story called "An Occurrence At Owl Creek Bridge." Did you happen to read that story, as a boy, perhaps?

IL DUCE. I don't know. Did he hear owls?

PIRANDELLO. I don't know if he heard owls or not. But in the story, a man is about to be hung, and they put the noose around his neck, but the rope breaks, he falls in the water and escapes, and makes his way home. Except at the last moment he realizes it's all been a fantasy that takes place in his mind in his final moments of life, and then his neck snaps and he dies, dangling from the rope, off Owl Creek Bridge. And that's why you hear owls.

IL DUCE. That makes no sense whatsoever. You're saying I'm being hung off a bridge?

PIRANDELLO. No. Maybe you're being shot and then hung upside down, like in her dream. The point is, in the moment before a person dies –

IL DUCE. But she's the one who dreamed about being hung upside down. So is it her dream, or mine?

PIRANDELLO. A play is the collective dream of the audience, a sort of crossroads, an intersection we gather at where everybody's dreams become one dream.

IL DUCE. So you're telling me I'm dead?

PIRANDELLO. Almost. Perhaps. It's a possibility.

IL DUCE. And this isn't real?

PIRANDELLO. That depends on how you look at it.

IL DUCE. I hear owls because being killed reminds me of a story which I may or may not have read when I was a boy? And this is like the intersection between my last hallucination and her dream and your – what? Your play?

PIRANDELLO. It could be that I'm writing a play in which you have this hallucination. Or it could be that she's dreaming that I'm writing a play in which these things are happening. Or –

THE ACTRESS. It does feel like a play. Or the discarded rough draft of a play. Maybe he's right. Maybe he's writing us. Or somebody is.

THE WIFE. Nobody is writing me.

THE ACTRESS. But how do you know? If it's not Pirandello's play, maybe it's God's play. Maybe God is also writing in order not to go mad.

IL DUCE. Too late for that, I think.

PIRANDELLO. Maybe all the time Il Duce thought he was writing his own play about Italy, I was writing a play about him which he came to the theatre late one night to ask me to write, while God, who is either imaginary or dead or both, was writing a play about both of us in blood on the underside of his coffin lid. And Il Duce's play about Italy and my play about him and God's play about us are all part of an infinite number of plays playing on an infinite series of interconnected stages, because time is not what keeps everything from happening at once – time IS everything happening at once, and that's why in her dream the last thing you said, before you died, was my name.

IL DUCE. I was telling her I'm actually Pirandello?

PIRANDELLO. You were telling her that nothing is real. That everything is like a play by Pirandello.

THE WIFE. God, I hate your plays. I've always hated your plays. They're smug and stupid and pretentious and dishonest, and they're an elaborate device to put you always one step ahead of everybody else. And all the time you were writing all these clever plays you were laying the groundwork for this horrible man to take power over our lives because you showed him that if you're just obnoxious enough you can prove to anybody that anything you want them to believe is true.

PIRANDELLO. That was not my intention. That was never my intention.

THE WIFE. You said Mussolini was the only person who could really understand your plays because he created his own reality and then got everybody else to believe in it. And look what happened. Look at all the horrible things that happened because people like you convince people who are dumber than you that whatever this monster does is all right because you want to think it's all right. But it isn't all right. And because I can see that, you call me crazy. Well, if that's what your reality is like, I'd rather live in a madhouse.

THE DAUGHTER. If I could only know just one true thing, before I die. Just one thing that I could be certain of. Then I think I could die in peace.

IL DUCE. But death is the one thing you can be certain of. No matter what Clara thinks I said in her dream, dying is truth. That's why Empedocles stepped in the volcano. Death is the ultimate verification of reality. Reality is what kills you. So maybe they are killing me, and hanging me upside down and calling me horrible names and spitting on my corpse. A part of me actually seems to remember that. But how can I remember it if I'm dead? And I'm pretty sure I never read that story about the owls. So how could I be haunted by owls in a story I never read? Or maybe I really am just an actor wearing a mask, playing a character I created called Mussolini. Or maybe I am Mussolini, but I'm not the Mussolini who is Il Duce. I'm the Mussolini inside him who was a nobody. And this other fellow, this character I've developed to hide behind, thought he was writing the play, but actually the play was writing him. And now I'm being written out, and these are the final, idiotic scenes in the play of my life. I hope there is a God, so he can forgive me for how badly I've played this role.

THE WIFE. If there is, he won't.

THE DAUGHTER. But if God won't forgive him, then who's going to forgive God? And who's going to forgive my father for writing a play in which his own daughter got so confused about what's real that now she doesn't know if he molested her or not?

THE WIFE. But it's true. He did molest you.

THE DAUGHTER. But how can I trust you? You're insane.

THE WIFE. All your life he's told you I was insane, but he's the one who keeps coming up with all these crazy ideas about nothing being real so he can hide from his own guilt for what he's done. Even an imaginary God is not going to forgive him for that.

PIRANDELLO. I'm a writer. Nobody will forgive me for anything, any more than I can forgive God for not existing. But God doesn't need our forgiveness. He doesn't give a shit about that. He's just trying to amuse himself, in his terrible loneliness, by writing a play. Then when he gets disgusted with it, he throws it in the fire and we all burn.

THE DAUGHTER. I don't think we can blame God for our own nightmares. Maybe the only truth we can ever know is our own nightmare. And this is mine.

THE WIFE. This is not your nightmare.

THE DAUGHTER. Then maybe it's yours, and you're having it in the madhouse where my father put you so nobody would believe you when you told them he molested me.

PIRANDELLO. I wanted to bring her home, but she preferred the reality she chose to believe, that I was a monster.

THE ACTRESS. Actually, I think it must be my dream. I am a creature of the theatre. That's all I've ever been, really. When I go outside the theatre, I'm nothing at all. This is exactly the sort of dream I'd have.

THE DAUGHTER. No, it's mine. It's definitely my nightmare.

IL DUCE. Well, if it's your nightmare, then please just tell us, once and for all, before somebody wakes up, did your father molest you, or didn't he?

THE DAUGHTER. I don't know. I thought it didn't happen, that it was just something my mother imagined, but now I keep having this eerie feeling that I really do remember it, and now I don't know if I'm just imagining that I remember it or if the memory was really in there all along, and I just didn't want to look at it.

PIRANDELLO. You can't remember something that never happened.

THE DAUGHTER. Of course I can. People do it all the time. But the things that feel most real are also the things that feel the most unreal. Like when we came out of the premiere of *Six Characters*, and the audience hated it so much. They were shouting horrible things at us. I was terrified they were going to tear us to pieces. It didn't seem like they just hated the play. They hated you for writing it, and me for being your daughter. They hated you for showing them that what they thought was real was a lie. And that hatred felt so real, and yet so completely unreal at the same time, like in stepping into the alley behind the theatre we had gone through the portal to another reality in which we were about to be torn to pieces by an angry mob, all because of a play you'd written.

PIRANDELLO. A play holds up the mirror to what people fear, and that terrifies them even more, and they want to destroy us to protect themselves from the truth.

THE DAUGHTER. I understand why they were so terrified, because that's my fear, too. That what you say in the play is true. That if you think something then it becomes real. Because my mother has repeated it to me so many times now I can never be sure if I actually remember it happening or I just remember her telling me over and over again that it happened. When you hear something repeated over and over again, if it's false, it starts to sound true, and if it's true, it starts to sound like a lie. Is it true, Papa? Is it true what she said?

PIRANDELLO. No. It's not true.

THE DAUGHTER. But how do you know?

PIRANDELLO. Because I know what the truth is.

THE DAUGHTER. Which truth? Which truth do you know? The truth you want to believe, or my mother's truth, or Il Duce's truth?

IL DUCE. Whatever the truth is, you probably don't want to know. But now I wonder if when God dies, when he's finally so ashamed of the mess he's created that he hangs himself off Owl Creek Bridge, what will his final word be?

THE DAUGHTER. Pirandello.

(The light fades on them and goes out.)

Notebook:
PIRANDELLO

I was born in Chaos, he said. Actually, Sicily. He moved to 15 Via Bosio in Rome and taught Italian literature and composition at a Teacher's College for women. Then he'd go home and write obsessively. He was wildly prolific, chain smoking cheap cigarettes as he worked. Each day he'd walk down the Via Nomentana to Porta Pia, and stop at the Caffé Aragano, on the Corso. He had two boys and a girl, and was especially close to his daughter. His wife, Antonietta, picked for him by his father, was intelligent and beautiful, but suffered from what Pirandello characterized as persecution mania. She thought Pirandello and everyone around her were conspiring against her, and was deeply jealous. In 1918 he finally put her in a mental institution, but found that he missed her so much, he changed his mind and determined to bring her home again. But she seems to have refused to leave the clinic.

He was a desperately lonely man. His initial attachment to his wife he gradually transferred first to his daughter and then to the actress Marta Abba. He said that when his daughter married and moved to Brazil he wanted to die. He felt things too deeply, and paid for it with a life of emotional torment that seems in its own way to have been as intense as his wife's. He wrote, he said, to keep from going mad.

Pirandello met Mussolini in person for the first time on October 22, 1923 at Palazzo Chigi. When, in 1925, he wanted to start his own theatre, he asked Mussolini for help and received some financial backing, but not enough to keep the theatre going for long. Mussolini attended the first performance at Pirandello's Art Theatre in 1925. Pirandello later lobbied to have his theatre made an official state theatre with a guaranteed budget, but his requests always seemed to disappear into the nightmare of the fascist bureaucracy. In fact, Mussolini was probably stringing him along, keeping him in line by giving him just enough hope.

At the first performance of *Six Characters In Search Of An Author* there were riots in the theatre, physical battles and shrieks of outrage in the audience, and people waiting outside the stage door screaming obscenities and threats at Pirandello and his terrified daughter. At the height of Pirandello's fame, the Lord Chamberlain tried to ban the play from production in England on the grounds that it was "too disturbing." The history of playwriting is also a history of institutional stupidity. The play was finally done in London, with great success, due largely to the efforts of George Bernard Shaw. Every playwright is always just one asshole away from oblivion.

Once, a performance of a play of mine had to be cancelled when an angry mob threatened to burn down the theatre. This production happened to be in India, but it might have been anywhere. It's difficult for me to understand how anybody's play could engender such behavior. What are they afraid of? By offering alternative views of reality, theatre seems to be a huge threat to persons who are convinced that only their view of reality can be tolerated. How about this: you come and see my play, I'll come and see yours, and then we'll have dinner and talk about it. Maybe we can actually learn something from each other. Then again, maybe not. Art should be an alternative to violence, not an excuse for it. But when the weak feel threatened, they get violent. Art is a lot more dangerous than you think.

In the tumultuous and chaotic, rough and tumble world of Italian politics after the First World War, Mussolini was one voice in a cluttered mess of opposition leaders eager for revolution which also included Marinetti and the Futurists, D'Annunzio and his followers from the Fiume expedition, and various socialist, anarchist and fascist groups. Mussolini had switched from socialism to fascism but was jealous of D'Annunzio, and also convinced of D'Annunzio's ultimate incompetence to lead such a movement. Mostly Mussolini was out to advance himself by any means necessary. He had no coherent body of principles except for a growing conviction that the ruthless bullies of the world would always prevail over those weakened by scruples and compassion.

Part of the way Mussolini achieved power in these early years was that he edited a popular newspaper in which he could mold public opinion and shape their view of reality, much as Fox News was later to do in America. And like Fox News, his paper was bankrolled by wealthy ultraconservatives who found him useful. Like Trump, Mussolini pretended to be a populist, but was always a tool of the wealthy class. Mussolini. Ubu the King. Trump. We must take into account the peculiar psychology of madmen.

After World War I, Mussolini developed a following by combining extreme nationalism with populist slogans and a promise of prosperity for all – strategies later adopted by American fascists. Pirandello thought Mussolini was in essence an actor who just pretended to be whatever he thought people wanted him to be.

As much as one is inclined to be sympathetic to Pirandello, if for nothing else, for the sake of his plays, one comes up against horrifying comments that make that difficult. In 1924 he said he had always had the greatest admiration for Mussolini, for what Pirandello called Mussolini's continuous creation of reality, a fascist reality which would not yield to anybody else's. Mussolini, he said, is one of the few people who understands that reality only exists in one's power to create it.

Not only is this statement chilling in itself, but it also casts a dark shadow on the very reason we might want to cut a fine writer some slack: he is praising Mussolini for understanding and putting into practice the central philosophical position of Pirandello's plays: that reality is something we fashion in our own minds, or in this case allow someone in power to fashion for us. Whatever other sympathies we may have for him, as a person and an artist, and however compelling his arguments are in the plays, the application of these ideas by a fascist government brings us directly to Orwell's *1984*, or Trump's America.

What is the relationship between Pirandello's sense of the elusive nature of reality and his willingness to support and enable a person like Mussolini, who lies as easily as he breathes and gets and keeps power by manipulating people's sense of reality? Pirandello saw reality as questionable, malleable. Did this make him more susceptible to the violent fantasy world of Mussolini's fascism? In the country, when it's dark, a man is easily deceived.

Did Deconstruction pave the way for the surreal world of lies that Trump and his fascist enablers offered as reality, like shit and onions on a plate? Deconstruction is, whatever else it may be, a primary tool of fascism. If anything can mean anything, then anything you want to believe is true, and whoever screams the loudest will eventually drill the lies they promulgate into the heads of the half-educated sheep who are their audience. Disassembling hierarchies is a good and necessary thing, and one of the main functions of art. But we should not lose sight of the fact that one who disassembles a hierarchy is always, whether they want to admit it or not, constructing a new hierarchy with themselves at the top. This is what many postmodern critics have done: they murder the author, then take his authority upon themselves, when in fact they are more often than not people incapable of creating much of anything but reams and reams of pretentious and confused bullshit. And whatever their intentions, they have made it easy for the right to assault the universities.

The right wing assault on higher education begins with the gradual defunding of state universities, where the children of most poor and middle class people have traditionally gotten their higher education, leading those institutions to raise tuition, and eventually creating a situation in which most people can't afford to send their children to college. And if they do go, they are often sentencing themselves to a lifetime of debt paying off student loans. This situation is a disgraceful obscenity which has been cynically created by a fascist oligarchy which needs a poorly educated population to maintain power. A liberal education is designed to help a person learn how to think critically, the way a good historian or scientist or journalist must. A vocational education may teach one how to fix your car or your plumbing or your computer, but without extended exposure to literature, history, science, psychology, art and philosophy a person is much less well equipped to defend themselves from manipulation by a corrupt, fascist media.

It was Pirandello's habit, from 1915 on, to shut himself up in his study and talk to the dead, or to imaginary people, perhaps the characters in his plays, perhaps others. When he had finally put his wife in a clinic, he missed her horribly, and looked forward to a time when he could have her home again. But at the last moment, she changed her mind and decided that she preferred her prison to living with her husband. Her supposed delusions about reality are the subtext and origin of many of his plays. Or was it a kind of madness she caught from him?

Why did his daughter try to kill herself? Was it because she was horrified at the terrible accusations her mother made? Or was there some truth in them? The irony is that a man who consistently asked how we can really know what is true, what is reality, would himself be tormented by another person's ambiguous sense of reality.

Reality is extremely unnatural. We live on the surface, deceiving ourselves, and not in the depths of our being. According to one eyewitness account, at the end of his life, Mussolini was living entirely in his dreams, had no contact with reality, had created his own fantastic world in his head, that his moods had no obvious connection to what was going on around him. Here, Ambrose Bierce keeps creeping into his head. We exist in a sort of twilight, on Owl Creek Bridge.

In 1952, in Dublin, Schrodinger told his audience that what he was about to say might sound like the ravings of a lunatic, but his Nobel Prize winning equations seem to be describing a number of different histories which are not alternatives but are all actually happening simultaneously. Later this idea would resurface as the Many Worlds Interpretation. Our existence is a series of interlocking realities, but we prefer appearance.

All autobiography is fragmented because all lives are fragmented. To enter a person's life is to move through a house of mirrors. In his journals, Hebbel describes a good play as an enormous building with as many rooms and corridors below ground as above. You can enter *King Lear* at any point, and at any point in your life, and no matter how many times you've read it, you still find rooms and corridors, attics and sub-basements you never knew existed, and all sorts of half forgotten treasures stored away there take on new significance.

William Carlos Williams and Ford Madox Ford are walking through a field, Ford characteristically expounding at length on literature and art. Later, Williams writes in his journal that Ford was so occupied with literary blather that he didn't even notice a sparrow they passed, terrified that they intended to harm its nest. But Ford's diary entry for that day is all about that sparrow and the three little birds in her nest. Even an exceptionally perceptive poet like Williams, blaming Ford for being oblivious to the sparrow's distress, hadn't a clue what was really going on in Ford's mind. For Pirandello, this is an illustration of one of the basic characteristics of human experience: we can never be sure we know what's actually going on inside anybody else. We usually don't even know for certain what's going on inside ourselves, or why.

The late romances of Shakespeare (*Pericles, Cymbeline, The Winter's Tale, The Tempest*) are a sort of cabinet of wonders in which reality is not what it seems, and fathers are often reunited with daughters and wives they thought were lost forever. Shakespeare wrote these plays just before moving back to Stratford, and I suspect they embody his longing to reconnect with his wife and daughters, as I suggested in *Loves Labours Wonne*. Pirandello and his Daughter are Prospero and Miranda reflected in broken mirrors.

Lost in the fog of the city. Old men should not look in the mirror. Too unreal. Or too much reality. I want to climb in the mirror with Alice. All memory is false memory. A person in the grip of a false memory is certain. The fake memory, perhaps implanted in childhood, becomes a part of their identity. To take away that false memory is to make their entire life a grotesque lie, so they clutch onto it, even though it may be a source of great misery for themselves and everyone around them. It is actually possible to die of loneliness. I used to think it was something that only happened in plays, but it turns out everything that happens in plays also happens sooner or later in real life – just in messier and more hopeless ways.

More and more, writing becomes like remembering something that happened to you in another life. In the play you were in backstage before you were in this one. An old playwright is left with a fistful of ashes. To be a writer you've got to learn to see in the dark.

Is Pirandello actually long dead, and Mussolini having a hallucination at the moment of his execution, or is Pirandello imagining the future as he writes a play in which events of his own life mix with his hopes and fears about Mussolini, and his complicity in Mussolini's fascist state? Or is it the Daughter's dream all along? Cocks crowing all night. Dragon flies. The Lady From The Sea. The only salvation, if any, comes from work.

The situation of the ghosts in Yeats' play *Purgatory* is not unlike that of the six characters in Pirandello's play. See also M. R. James: "The Ash Tree." Ambrose Bierce: "An Occurrence At Owl Creek Bridge." Empedocles. McTaggart. Eliot. Bradley's *Appearance And Reality*. Kott's *The Eating Of The Gods*. Study the inhabitants of the ash tree out your window. Spiders, spiders, spiders.

Every house is a labyrinth of interlocking stages upon which are played out over time a multitude of contradictory realities and unresolved ambiguities. Truth is not a jest. Madness is highly contagious. We are puppets at a masquerade. A pistol shot in the garden.

In the prehistoric rituals which were most likely the first theatrical performances, the gods themselves were the audience. The ritual was performed to persuade the gods to do certain things that would benefit mankind. God is in the audience tonight. No pressure, but if he gives us a bad review, the show closes forever.

At night before I fall asleep I hear voices, as if I were hearing them on an old transistor radio in my head. My beloved was swallowed by an elevator. This is about a mirror and its fragments. I am not interested in your syphilitic sister.

Mussolini's fortune is read: the Hanged Man. Pirandello is the Fool. Dove or raven? Which are you? I am well acquainted with strangeness. In this place of darkness.

Astolfo copulating with the Hippogriff. Orlando mad. We are all lost in the forest. Reading Italian literature, which has resisted me stubbornly for years, and suddenly, after years of not quite connecting, I realize I am home.

There's somebody in the White Church. Lights moving at night in the White Church. Somebody laughing in there. God laughing in the White Church. Or maybe the Devil. Time is jumbled there. Most of everything is hidden, or in fragments. Someone burying something in a field. Little hand carved coffins full of dolls with staring eyes.

What is the relationship of solitude to disinterest? Detachment? Is the price of truth self denial? Pieces of my soul keep dropping off and falling into the mud puddles on the dirty, uneven brick road. What we find when we reach the Emerald City is death.

Lost in a vast labyrinth, surrounded by unfathomable mystery. We tell ourselves that God is light. But what if God is darkness?

What is at the core of the apple, the core of the soul? Thought is best when the mind is gathered into herself, when one is at home, in a little castle in the soul. Plato and Meister Eckhart. At the moment of division between past and future, where there is nothing. Passion does not satisfy desire.

I realized I had been staring at my hands. And I thought, suddenly, whose hands are these? What is the relationship between what seems to be outside my skin, and what seems to be inside it? Can we draw boundaries where we want? When space is set apart, as in the magic circle of the theatre, a universe comes into being. We are an uncanny reconstruction. To be born is a re-entry into form. A play is a portal to another dimension.

All is possible. All is mutability. Is there a reality independent of how the universe appears to us? This statement is false. Which is how we know it's true. He weeps by the side of the ocean. He weeps at the top of the hill. God has written a book of nonsense.

I am the Other Passenger. I am a geographer of nonsense. I illuminate imaginary topographies, from Highgate to San Remo and back. An Albanian is conspiring with my cat to drive me mad.

Bruno's works on memory are full of references to magic. The art of memory as a mystical magic technique. If you don't study the past, you have no future. You're just an ordinary circus clown.

On his death bed, Pirandello, in a state of semi-delirium, and apparently writing a play in his head, said, "Yes. An olive tree in the center of the stage. That's the answer!" Possibly he was having a prevision of *Waiting For Godot*.

You walk and walk all night, and then you come to a door. And somehow you know that this door has been waiting there for you since you were born. And you must decide, do I open the door, or do I keep walking, knowing I might never find this door again? Or do I just lie down here like a dog in front of the door and die? Eventually everybody ends up at Kafka's door.

Wittgenstein had seven grand pianos in his house. Jimmy Casey had a barn full of pianos, stacked up to the ceiling. At Ohio State, around 1970, an efficiency expert hired by the university reported that a great way to save money and space would be to get rid of all the pianos. Or, on the other hand, it might be a better idea to save money by strangling the efficiency expert with piano wire.

I am suffering, he said, from a fatal case of mythology: the compulsive telling of tales. You can't understand the beginning until you've seen the end, and then it's too late. You are made of what you're trying to understand. You are the play you're writing. To understand anything you've got to draw a distinction, separate yourself from what you're studying. So we're always dealing in fragments.

Northrop Frye suggests that one indication of a masterpiece is that it seems to draw us to a point at which we become aware of an enormous number of converging patterns of significance. Frye says myth is a structural element in literature because literature is displaced mythology. Blake raises the question of the reality of the poetic vision, neither objective nor subjective but rather brought into existence by the act of creation itself. Myth, ritual, symbol, archetype: entanglement.

That creative imagination might transform the universe is or should be a good thing – a way to save ourselves from the nightmare science presents to us as reality. Art does this. And art is a good thing. In some ways it is the best of us. But the imagination of the stupid and evil can be used to manipulate, control and destroy.

We enter a play as if stumbling into an enormous, complex ancient castle with many floors, stairways, sub-basements and towers. I dream of such places, and have since I was a child. In my dreams I wander in a gigantic, multi-dimensional labyrinth, as in God's brain. Each step I take I am followed by the panther woman. Click click click. Fear death by water. She that was lost whilst wandering over the bogs in search of mysterious lights.

Subsequent justifications are usually crap, and things are always more interesting when taken out of context and imperfectly revealed. But what is taken out of context must then be put back again and seen differently because of what you've learned by doing so.

Appearance and reality. Consequences. Re-entry into the form. To retrace a step, he said, can be considered not to have taken it. But only in a pure world of mathematics. You have crossed a boundary. Now see how difficult it is to go back.

I am the dirty joke you shared with God. I am the man in the moon. An olive tree in the center of the stage. That's the answer. Everything is real. Nothing is real. Some things are more real than others. That which is most real also feels the most unreal. Everything, said Evreinov, is theatre, including animals, plants, and, I suppose, inanimate objects. We came into being as the result of a useless accident, and we'll end the same way.

In 1963, Jean-Luc Godard, Alberto Moravia, Brigitte Bardot, Jack Palance, Curzio Malaparte and Fritz Lang are all sitting on a terrace of the house Malaparte designed at Capri, looking at the ocean, watching the sun set and talking about life. One of them mentions Pirandello. Which one?

It's difficult to take the position that all "truths" are equally valid when confronted with Auschwitz. At this extreme point of human experience, to take the position that denying the reality of what happened there is as valid a position as accepting it is not just ridiculous – it's despicable. So what are we to make of Pirandello's plays, and of his life?

Pirandello said that reality is ephemeral, can vanish at any moment, and not everybody is capable of creating a reality for himself, so they need somebody to make a reality for them. Mussolini was a person happy to make a reality for them. It is more than a little reminiscent of the argument of the Grand Inquisitor.

My childhood was in great measure inhabited by puppets and marionettes. I had a Howdy Doody marionette, a Clarabell the Clown marionette, a Jerry Mahoney dummy, and a collection of hand puppets, mostly Howdy Doody characters (Clarabell, Howdy, Phineas T. Bluster, Dilly Dally). Also a Mickey Mouse hand puppet I got in Pittsburgh. Two of these were purchased. One was given to Carolee, one to me. Carolee cried because she wanted mine, although they were identical. I offered to trade with her. Then she cried because she said I was trying to take her puppet. Then she wanted both of them. Then she wanted neither of them. What she really wanted, of course, was for me to be run over by a streetcar. She simply resented my presence altogether. This was my introduction to certain experiences I would have later in my life.

All remembrance is imperfect. It's never perfectly clear how much of memorial reconstruction is in fact imagination. Eyewitness testimony is often demonstrably wrong. Lives have been ruined by the imperfect memories of persons who are convinced they know what reality is. The best one can hope for is small islands of calm in the midst of wild confusion. God is made of lies.

On the wall in the living room, a gigantic painting of Custer's Last Stand which had perhaps fallen off a truck in New Jersey. An incredible mass of grisly detail. Custer grew up near where I live, not far from my Lemasters family, descendants of Huguenot refugees, near some Lenne Lenape, perhaps also my relatives from the Indian scout Snowden line. A child in Phoenix, I stand in Marie's living room looking at that painting while Sinatra records play. Her father made good sauce, but different from my grandmother's. Pynchon feeding pigeons in Vineland.

One rainy evening at a seaside inn, Max Ernst stares at the pattern in the floorboards and sees God's face. (A fleeting memory of being God.) Ernst said collage is the coupling of two realities. A village in the Rhine. (The Lorelei, the postcard pictures in the little plastic red television clicker toy Gus and Dot brought from Germany). It still sits on my desk as I write. When I get discouraged, I pick it up and take a voyage down the Rhine.

Ernst, told by an older artist upset by his work, "You have too much talent. You should use less of it." Gently reproducing that which saw itself in me, Ernst says. He mentions Vasari's story about the painter who stared for hours at a wall people had been spitting on, seeing magnificent landscapes there. I've stumbled upon several different versions of this observation in the last few weeks, all by accident. The work creates itself. You pick out and project what sees itself in you.

Sense memory. Emotion memory. Hypnagogic visions. Automatic writing. Yeats. We come to bring you metaphors for poetry.

I have done everything to render my soul monstrous, said Rimbaud. How many gentlemen have you lost in this action? She smells like rabbit fur after rain.

"I spoke the truth, straight from my heart. I believe that is always madness." – Sheridan Le Fanu, *The Rose And The Key*.

A rainy day in 1949. Love memories, visions of half sleep, Dylan Thomas, remembering Christmas in Wales, speaks of the voices he hears before he drifts off to sleep. I'm interested in these voices, which I also hear, how common they are, if writers hear them more often than others, where they come from, and how they are related to the voices one hears when writing. Lying in bed on Christmas Eve, couldn't sleep, heard muffled voices from the living room, and the mass from Rome. What is the mechanism of collage? An image of one's hallucination transformed into dramas.

The voices Dylan Thomas heard as a child before he went to sleep. The voices I heard, and still hear. The Kaleidoscope girl warned me: "Never speak of those voices when any medical professional can overhear you. They'll put you in a straight jacket and lock you up in a padded cell. Those people can only think clinically. They don't understand people who create. Stay away from them." I think it was excellent advice. Dylan Thomas was deeply influenced by Bram Stoker's *Dracula*. There are many interconnections we could not have imagined, but which make perfect sense in retrospect. Plays, said Okkie Brownstein, are just like that.

Can two mutually exclusive realities be true? What about an infinite number of mutually exclusive realities? You change your mind so quickly and get angry so suddenly, nobody can keep up with you. One writes in order not to go mad. And one fails.

Meister Eckhart said that no man ever gave up so much in this life that he could not find something else to let go. We accumulate, and then we lose. Objects, people, animals, ourselves. We assemble ourselves over the years like a cabinet of curiosities and then gradually lose everything we have. First we become this accumulation. Then we become this loss. Eventually, we become nothing. If it be nothing, I won't need my spectacles.

Why are people so horrible? she said. Because we're made in God's image. God is a bowl of spaghetti in my grandmother's kitchen. Or a house full of ticking clocks that all say different times. God is Larry Parks' dream. Love is the only salvation, but all who love are damned.

The relationship of capitalism to natural selection: both are manifestations of the same inexorable process: the murder of the weaker by the stronger. This is a strange business, said Molière, making honest people laugh. Is Storr correct that it's the discrepancy between the outer and inner worlds that drives the creative imagination? We spend our lives interacting with symbolic animals. With ghosts.

Travel is a surreal experiment. The goal of art is to make the real strange and the strange real. The artist listens to voices in the dark, but so do madmen and murderers. The voices in the dark are the subconscious. A deep connection to the subconscious, the source of imagination, can result in *King Lear*. On the other hand, opening one's self up to one's subconscious can lead to bigotry, hate, and fascism. An artist must use his gift of being able to access the deepest recesses of his subconscious to create, not to destroy, or to apologize for those who would destroy.

Max Ernst, Octavio Paz and Susan Howe all are sitting in a room full of ticking clocks. Then the clocks all begin to strike. What time is it? Too late. We look at everything through broken windows and in cracked mirrors.

Edward Bond says we prove the world real by dying in it. A perverted version of this observation is Mussolini's justification for murder: he is helping people understand what's real. In ending the lives of others he is asserting the victory of his own reality. He imposes it upon others, and the proof of it is that he can kill them. The greatest villains steal the truth and use it to tell lies.

Larry Parks' dream, from *Canticle For Goats* (actually my dream):

You're in a theatre. In the wings. Loud music. A burlesque show. A chorus line of fat ladies in red silk dresses and black garters. They kick like a row of elephants and they all have mustaches and little beards. Backstage, old men are playing poker. The fat ladies lumber off. The music ends. The old men sit very still, listening. There is no applause. No rustle. No cough. There is absolutely no sound. One of the old men rises. The others won't look at him. It is his show. He puts on his coat and hat and goes out into the alley. The other old men shake their heads and mumble. The stage manager goes to the curtain and looks out. My god, he says. My god. Young people are carrying stretchers past you. On the stretchers are bodies covered with sheets. Pinned to the left side of each body is a small piece of paper, spattered with blood. You go through the curtain and onto the stage. The audience is nearly full. They all sit up straight. They do not move. Their necks all end in bloody stumps. They have no heads. There are rows and rows of headless bodies sitting straight up in front of you. Each has a small piece of paper, spattered with blood, pinned to the left side of its chest. The young people are methodically placing the stiff, headless bodies on stretchers and carrying them away from you. The theatre is cold. You hear someone screaming far away. You wonder who it can be. Then you realize: It is Larry Parks. Larry Parks is screaming.

subconscious can lead to bigotry, hate, and fascism. An artist must use his gift of being able to access the deepest recesses of his subconscious to create, not to destroy, or to apologize for those who would destroy.

Max Ernst, Octavio Paz and Susan Howe all are sitting in a room full of ticking clocks. Then the clocks all begin to strike. What time is it? Too late. We look at everything through broken windows and in cracked mirrors.

Edward Bond says we prove the world real by dying in it. A perverted version of this observation is Mussolini's justification for murder: he is helping people understand what's real. In ending the lives of others he is asserting the victory of his own reality. He imposes it upon others, and the proof of it is that he can kill them. The greatest villains steal the truth and use it to tell lies.

Larry Parks' dream, from *Canticle For Goats* (actually my dream):

You're in a theatre. In the wings. Loud music. A burlesque show. A chorus line of fat ladies in red silk dresses and black garters. They kick like a row of elephants and they all have mustaches and little beards. Backstage, old men are playing poker. The fat ladies lumber off. The music ends. The old men sit very still, listening. There is no applause. No rustle. No cough. There is absolutely no sound. One of the old men rises. The others won't look at him. It is his show. He puts on his coat and hat and goes out into the alley. The other old men shake their heads and mumble. The stage manager goes to the curtain and looks out. My god, he says. My god. Young people are carrying stretchers past you. On the stretchers are bodies covered with sheets. Pinned to the left side of each body is a small piece of paper, spattered with blood. You go through the curtain and onto the stage. The audience is nearly full. They all sit up straight. They do not move. Their necks all end in bloody stumps. They have no heads. There are rows and rows of headless bodies sitting straight up in front of you. Each has a small piece of paper, spattered with blood, pinned to the left side of its chest. The young people are methodically placing the stiff, headless bodies on stretchers and carrying them away from you. The theatre is cold. You hear someone screaming far away. You wonder who it can be. Then you realize: It is Larry Parks. Larry Parks is screaming.

The Recollection of Green Rain

A Play

by Don Nigro

CHARACTERS

WALTER MAP – a writer
AGNES – a young woman

SETTING

A house by the woods.

TIME

Late twelfth century England.

AUTHOR'S NOTES

Walter Map (1140-c1210) was a Welsh collector of anecdotes, trivia, folklore, and some actual history, which he assembled in a volume which, centuries later, was translated by the great author of ghost stories M. R. James. Along with another avid collector of curiosities, William of Newburgh, Map recorded, among many other odd and bizarre things, the first stories of English vampires. It was William of Newburgh who told the story of the two mysterious green children who appeared inexplicably in Woolpit, Suffolk, during the reign of King Stephen, also mentioned by Robert Burton in *The Anatomy Of Melancholy*. They spoke an unknown language and at first would only eat broad beans. The boy died soon after being baptized, but the girl was taken in by the family of Sir Richard de Caine of Wykes and eventually married. She insisted she was from St Martin's Land, a subterranean world inhabited by green people. As her diet expanded she gradually lost her green color. She was considered somewhat wanton in her behavior. There is no record of Walter Map ever having met her.

(**WALTER MAP**, *a writer, sits with* **AGNES**, *a young woman, in the kitchen of a small house by the woods in England, in the late twelfth century.*)

MAP. Do you remember?

AGNES. Less and less. Sometimes it's like waking up after you've had an extremely vivid dream. It was so real. It was the only thing that was real. And then you wake up and you're someplace else and you can feel the dream slipping away, and you know that once it's gone, you'll never be able to get back there. Sometimes I dream about it. My brother comes to me in dreams. He asks me to come back with him.

MAP. Back where?

AGNES. To the other place. To where we came from.

MAP. What kind of place was it?

AGNES. It was underground, mostly. Caves and tunnels under the earth.

MAP. How did you see?

AGNES. With our eyes.

MAP. But it must have been dark there, in caves and tunnels.

AGNES. We had torches. But there were places where there was light.

MAP. Light from where?

AGNES. I don't know. Maybe there were cracks in the earth. Maybe something was growing there that gave off light. It was caves and tunnels, but there was light.

Some places were very dark. Some places here are very dark. There is much darkness everywhere. But there is some light.

MAP. What did you do there?

AGNES. We tended the herds.

MAP. What sort of herds? Cows? Sheep?

AGNES. Something like sheep. But not exactly. The babies were soft, like lambs. But different. Our job was to look for strays. That's what we were doing, I suppose, when we came up into the light. To this place. My brother and I.

MAP. You suppose?

AGNES. I don't remember exactly how we got here. But I remember we suddenly came up into the light. Not dim light, like below, but bright light. It nearly blinded us. My brother was afraid and wanted to go back. But we'd somehow stumbled into the Wolfpits. And then some people found us. And they were asking us questions in a language we didn't understand.

MAP. What language did you speak?

AGNES. Not English. We spoke some other language in the other place, under the earth.

MAP. Sir Richard said it sounded to him like Flemish.

AGNES. Did he?

MAP. Yes.

AGNES. I don't know what Flemish sounds like. Does Sir Richard speak Flemish?

MAP. No. He just thought it sounded like Flemish. Or what he imagined Flemish would sound like.

AGNES. What he imagined.

MAP. That's what he said.

AGNES. So you've been talking to Sir Richard about me?

MAP. I spoke to him because he's the one who took you in.

AGNES. Yes. He took us in.

MAP. He seems like a kind man. Was he kind to you?

AGNES. It was kind of him to take us in.

MAP. Can you say something to me, in your other language?

AGNES. No. I've forgotten it now. Sometimes I can almost remember. It's like it's a place that's just off the edge of the map. Your name is Map.

MAP. Yes.

AGNES. Walter Map.

MAP. Yes.

AGNES. My recollection is just off your edge, Walter. Did Sir Richard tell you I'm a wicked girl?

MAP. He said you were an unusual girl.

AGNES. When they first found us, some of them thought we were devils. Demons. Not human. They thought we should be burned. But there was a meeting, and it was decided that we should be baptized instead. That if the holy water didn't burn us, we probably weren't devils. Then my brother died. But it wasn't the holy water that killed him. We were different. That's what killed him. To be different, you see. To be always misunderstood. To not know for sure what you are. Everyone looks at you and misunderstands. But you can't explain.

MAP. How were you different?

AGNES. Well, for one thing, we were green. Our skin was green. They called us the Green Children.

MAP. You're not green now.

AGNES. Are you disappointed? At first we'd only eat a certain kind of raw beans. But gradually we learned to eat your food, and the green began to fade. The only thing left of the green now is my eyes, and they're changing color, too. Soon there'll be nothing left.

MAP. What else do you remember, about the world you came from?

AGNES. I remember the rain. It used to rain.

MAP. In the caves?

AGNES. There were open places. Where the sheep grazed. The caves led to open places, and then back deep underground, but there were places where it rained, and the rain was green. I dream about green rain.

MAP. Have you ever tried looking for the cave?

AGNES. Yes. Sir Richard took us back to the Wolfpits, but we couldn't find the cave. There were caves there, of a sort, but they didn't seem to lead anywhere. I used to look at my hands and I could see the green fading away. I'd look in the mirror and see the face of this girl, this stranger, and the green was fading away. It was like I was fading away. That soon I'd be a ghost. That's what they call western people in the far east: ghosts. Sir Richard told me that. A sailor told him. He was full of that sort of information. But that's what I felt like. Like I was turning into a ghost. What do you really think of me? You're being polite, but what do you actually think of me? Don't lie to me. If you lie to me I won't tell you anything more.

MAP. I think you made up a story, when you were a child, and gradually you came to like the story better than the truth.

AGNES. But how could it be a story? We were green. Many people saw us. Many can testify to this fact. So if our story was just a story, how do you explain that?

MAP. I have no explanation.

AGNES. But you don't believe about the cave.

MAP. And the things which are not quite sheep, and the light beneath the earth, and the green rain. That's very difficult to believe. But I can understand that as a child –

AGNES. How sad your life must be. Going about the countryside. Writing down lies. That is what you do, isn't it? That's why you're talking to me.

MAP. I am a collector of information. Of stories.

AGNES. And what do you do with these stories?

MAP. Write them down, and eventually make a book of them.

AGNES. A book of lies?

MAP. Some of the stories are true, as far as I'm able to determine. Some of them are legends and tales that almost certainly are not true, but are interesting as legends and tales. I try not to pass judgement. I just tell the story as I heard it.

AGNES. So you don't distinguish between truth and lies.

MAP. Lies are only another form of truth. The truth is what actually is the case. What you call a lie can be a story which although not itself literally true, reveals something else about experience or human nature that is true. The truth content of a lie is sometimes what it reveals about the liar.

AGNES. And what do my lies reveal to you about me?

MAP. That you have a secret. Probably one a good bit less fantastic than the tale you tell to hide it. Maybe there was a cave. Some sort of cave. I expect the green color came from lack of sunlight and a peculiar diet, combined with perhaps a naturally slightly olive complexion, like that of, say gypsies or Italians. People who are habitually telling stories.

AGNES. But you're a writer. You're a person who's habitually telling stories. So why are you better than me?

MAP. I never said I was better than you.

AGNES. But you're judging me. How can you judge me if you do the same thing you think I do, and write it down?

MAP. But I'm not judging you. You asked me to honestly tell you what I really thought, and I told you, and you're the one who's judging me for judging you, when all I'm doing is listening to what you say.

AGNES. And writing it down.

MAP. I will write it down, yes.

AGNES. And put it in a book.

MAP. Very likely.

AGNES. So you're profiting from writing down my lies.

MAP. Nobody forced you to speak with me.

AGNES. And nobody forced you to come all this way to talk to me.

MAP. No. I wanted to talk to you.

AGNES. Why? You must have come a long ways out of your way to get here. Why would you go to all of that trouble just to talk to a girl you must have already decided was insane or a liar before you even met me?

MAP. Because the story is so fascinating. Two children found by a wolf pit, not understanding English, speaking a language that nobody can understand, wearing a style of clothing nobody had ever seen before, and they're green. And when the surviving girl learns to talk, she tells a story about coming from a land under the earth, where they raise animals which are both sheep and not sheep. Now, that's a story.

AGNES. What other things are you putting in your book? Are you just focusing on green people, or are you also interested in people with stripes?

MAP. I'm interested in curiosities.

AGNES. So that's what I am to you? A curiosity?

MAP. You are a human being. Your story is a curiosity.

AGNES. But how do you know?

MAP. How do I know what?

AGNES. How do you know I'm a human being?

MAP. It's obvious that you're a human being.

AGNES. How is it obvious? You haven't seen me naked. How do you know I don't have an extra set of teeth in my navel, and a tail like a monkey? That would be a curiosity.

MAP. I think, given the best evidence I have, you appear to most likely be a human being. Do you believe you're not a human being?

AGNES. I don't know what I am. That's the problem. But I don't think I want to be treated like some sort of monster in your book.

MAP. I don't think you're a monster. You're clearly quite intelligent, you have a lot of spirit, a good deal of complexity in your disposition, a sense of humor, and you're not disposed to let me get away with anything. I find much to admire in that.

AGNES. Don't patronize me.

MAP. I'm not patronizing you.

AGNES. But how do I know? How do I know you're not lying to me, just to get on my good side, so I'll keep giving you all this bizarre material to put in your stupid book?

MAP. I promise to tell the story exactly as you tell it to me.

AGNES. But what good is the promise of a writer? A writer is a person who is by definition a liar. The minute you write something down, it's a lie, because it can't possibly be what it's trying to pretend it is. It's just a bunch of words.

MAP. I'm just trying to understand.

AGNES. But you can't understand. I don't understand. The people in this village don't understand each other. Or themselves, for that matter. How can they understand a girl they found in a wolf pit who speaks gibberish and is green?

MAP. Maybe I can't understand. But if I write down your story, maybe somebody will read it who can.

AGNES. You have no idea how it feels to be so alone. When I dream about it, about that place, it's like looking into a green marble. It's so beautiful. They said my brother was sick but I think he starved himself because he missed the Green World so much. It's always fatal to really, really miss something. Some person. Some place. The more you care, the worse it is. Love kills you. The world belongs to those who don't give a shit.

MAP. That is an extremely vulgar expression. Did you just invent it?

AGNES. Apparently. Do you like it?

MAP. Yes, actually. There is a place for vulgarity.

AGNES. Where? In Hell?

MAP. Well, yes.

AGNES. Is this Hell then?

MAP. No, this is England. Hell is further south. Closer to London.

AGNES. Maybe that's where I've come from. Maybe I'm a demon come from Hell to torment people like you. People who feed off other people like vampires.

MAP. Actually, I've written about vampires. They're really quite interesting. The vampire –

AGNES. Have you ever made love to a green girl?

MAP. No. I'm fairly sure I haven't.

AGNES. Why not?

MAP. Because I only know one green girl, and she's not green. Except for her eyes, just a bit, in a certain light.

AGNES. That's tragic. Where did you get a stupid name like Map?

MAP. From my father.

AGNES. And Walter is also a pretty stupid name. It's just a syllable away from being Walnut. Walnut Map. Actually that's a better name for you. The story of the Green Girl, by Walnut Map.

MAP. What was your name in the green world? Certainly not Agnes.

AGNES. No. In the Green World we only have secret names. So I can't tell you. I want to, but I can't. I've sworn a vow. If I break it, I'll be banished from the Green World forever. And I really want to go back. But I don't know how to get there. They seem to have closed the portal we came out of. Do you know what I need? I need a map. I need a map to help me find my way home. But there are no maps to the Green World. Just people who point you in the wrong direction. Because we don't like tourists in the Green World. We kill them, cut them up in pieces and make stew out of them. And we eat this stew with big chunks of fresh baked bread smeared all over with apple butter.

MAP. It sounds like a lovely place.

AGNES. Would you like to come? Because you can come with me if you'd like. If you dare. Do you care to come with me, Walter?

MAP. What about your husband? Is he coming too?

AGNES. My husband?

MAP. You have a husband, don't you?

AGNES. Do I?

MAP. I was told you did. Wouldn't your husband object to me coming with you to find the Green World?

AGNES. I don't actually consider this world to be real. It's the other world that matters. The person you refer to as my husband is someone Sir Richard paid to marry me before I became impregnated by one of the village boys. Sir Richard found me rather a lot to handle once I grew up a little. He couldn't control me. So he did what men do when they have a horse they can't control. They sell her.

MAP. But if Sir Richard paid your husband, he didn't sell you. He paid somebody to take you.

AGNES. Are you trying to make me feel worse?

MAP. No. I'm trying to understand you.

AGNES. Even if this world is real, my marriage isn't. It's just a piece of paper. I refuse to recognize the validity of any union sanctified by a financial transaction. So what's your verdict? Do you think I'm a liar, or do you think I'm insane?

MAP. I think you're lost.

AGNES. Of course I'm lost. That's why I need a map. For a moment there I was actually imagining what it might be like to make love with you. But I don't think I could love a man who wasn't green.

MAP. But there isn't anybody who's green.

AGNES. If I kiss a Prince does he turn into a frog? Or does that only work the other way? And in any case, who would want to kiss a Prince? Well, you might. You certainly don't seem to find me attractive.

MAP. I find you extremely attractive. Pretty much every man in the village does, from what I hear. But, sadly, none of us are green.

AGNES. I could marry my brother.

MAP. Even if you weren't already married, you couldn't marry your brother.

AGNES. Why not?

MAP. Because he's your brother. And because he's dead.

AGNES. But dead brothers make the best husbands. In the Green World we always marry our brothers. Except for those who marry their sisters. But the most convenient sort of brother is a dead brother. Except they come back to haunt you. My brother haunts me. I dream about him every night. He visits me in my dreams and tells me to come home. It's so lonely here. I don't like this place. I want to go back. Can you help me?

MAP. All I can do is write about you.

AGNES. Will you make me sound crazy?

MAP. All interesting people sound a little crazy.

AGNES. Walter Map, why won't you take me away to the Green World? I can tell by the way you look at me that you want me. We'll cuddle up with the creatures who are not quite sheep and make love in the green rain.

MAP. That's a very tempting offer. It really is. But I can't. I've taken vows.

AGNES. You're a priest?

MAP. I'm a prebendary.

AGNES. A prebendary? What the hell is that? Is that like a dromedary? You're some sort of camel?

MAP. A member of the minor clergy. And I can't be running off with anybody's wife. However charming she may be.

AGNES. You're sure?

MAP. Sadly, yes.

AGNES. All right. Then I forbid you to write about me.

MAP. You forbid me?

AGNES. You owe it to me. You have chosen not to save me, coward that you are, and take me to the Green World. Therefore I am owed this. Swear to me on your immortal soul, if writers have souls, which I rather doubt, but nevertheless, swear to me that you will never write about me. If you love me, you'll swear.

MAP. Others will write about you, if I don't.

AGNES. I'm not talking about others. I'm talking about you. If you love me, you'll swear.

MAP. All right. I swear.

AGNES. So you do love me.

MAP. I've sworn. You can make of it what you like.

AGNES. And when you break your promise, as you certainly will, remember me, and feel ashamed.

MAP. Why are you so certain I'll break my promise?

AGNES. Because you're a man. And because you're a writer. And because for the rest of your life you'll always regret that you didn't run off with me when you had the chance. And you'll feel so lonely and unhappy that you'll write about me, because writing is what people do to try and forget that they're going to die and everything they love is going to die. And when you betray me, the cock will crow, and you'll be very, very ashamed of yourself, but you'll keep writing, because you don't have anything else. Because I'll be gone. And maybe you'll even change your mind and come back for me, but I won't be here. Because somebody braver than you will have carried me off to look for the Green World. Or I'll be dead. Because I'm dying, too, just like my brother. This is what we die of. We die for the recollection of green rain.

MAP. I'm sorry that you're unhappy. I wish there was something I could do.

AGNES. The best thing you can do is go away.

MAP. All right.

(Pause.)

Well. It's been a pleasure speaking with you.

AGNES. Just shut up and go.

MAP. All right.

AGNES. You want me so much. Do you think I can't see it? All of you men are like this. Sir Richard wasn't just afraid the village boys would get me pregnant. He didn't trust himself with me. I could see it in his eyes. He desired me, and he feared the power it gave me over him. So he paid someone to take me out of his sight. But I'm still in his head. Sometimes he rides by and looks at the house. But he won't come in. He never comes in. Men are such pathetic cowards. And you're just the same. But it doesn't matter. I wouldn't have you anyway. I just want to torture you. Because you all think you're saving me, but you're not saving me. You're controlling me and stealing from me. You've taken away my soul. I'm nobody now. I don't belong here and I can't get back to where I've come from. I'm nobody. All I can do is die.

MAP. Listen to me. When Sir Richard said the language you spoke, the one you've forgotten, sounded to him like Flemish, something occurred to me. Do you know that around the time you and and your brother were found, there was a terrible massacre of Flemish immigrants by the local people. Not here, but not that far away. They were taken to a dark place and slaughtered in the rain. And I wondered if perhaps two children might have –

AGNES. I am from the Green World.

MAP. Might have been wandering for some time, and when a person is malnourished, their skin can turn a sort of grayish color, and certain hallucinations brought on by starvation and emotional trauma –

AGNES. I AM FROM THE GREEN WORLD UNDER THE EARTH. AND NONE OF THIS IS REAL. NONE OF IT.

MAP. *(Reaching out his hand to touch her back.)* Perhaps –

AGNES. If you touch me, I'll scream. Get out. Go write your stories. Go write about vampires and other curiosities. Try and forget me if you can. But at night, when you're lying alone in bed, you'll dream about me. Even when you're very old you'll dream about me. You'll dream about me naked in green rain.

> *(They look at each other. The light fades on them and goes out.)*

Pinocchio

A Play

by Don Nigro

CHARACTERS

GLORIA – a young woman
PINOCCHIO – a puppet

SETTING

A table at an Italian restaurant. Spaghetti and wine.

(**PINOCCHIO** *and* **GLORIA** *at a table in an Italian restaurant.*)

GLORIA. So. Enough about me. I've been going on and on about myself. Men usually don't like you doing that. They're always interrupting so they can perpetuate the illusion that they're in charge. But you've been a remarkably good listener. I really admire that in a man. I think it's an indication of strength. That's very attractive. So, tell me about yourself.

PINOCCHIO. Well. My name is Pinocchio. And I'm a puppet.

GLORIA. You're what?

PINOCCHIO. A puppet.

GLORIA. What do you mean?

PINOCCHIO. I'm a puppet.

GLORIA. You're a puppet?

PINOCCHIO. You didn't notice?

GLORIA. Well, to be honest, I'm a little nearsighted, but I don't usually wear my glasses on a first date because it doesn't make the best impression. That's vanity. I know. I need to work on that. But I can't wear contacts because I just can't stand anything touching my eyeballs. I guess I have anxiety issues or something but it totally freaks me out. You know what I mean?

PINOCCHIO. My eyes were carved and then painted.

GLORIA. Your eyes were – oh, I see. Because you're a puppet.

PINOCCHIO. Yes.

GLORIA. So, when you say you're a puppet, is this like, some sort of a metaphor?

PINOCCHIO. No. I'm not a metaphor. I'm a puppet.

GLORIA. So, like, you've got somebody's giant hand up your ass, or –

PINOCCHIO. No. I'm not a hand puppet. Obviously. I'm a marionette.

GLORIA. So, you've got, like strings? Because I don't see any strings.

PINOCCHIO. No. I've got no strings. I don't need any strings. I'm a puppet who's come to life.

GLORIA. Uh huh.

(Pause.)

Well, that's different.

(Pause.)

So, uh, have you always been a puppet?

PINOCCHIO. Actually, no. I started out as a piece of wood. Sometimes I dream that I'm still part of an oak tree. In my dream, I can actually feel the sap running. It's really very comforting, like hearing your mother's heart beat and blood flowing in the womb must be for, you know, meat people.

GLORIA. Meat people?

PINOCCHIO. People made of meat. Like you. Although some of us prefer the term "meat puppets" because they believe that actually everybody is puppets. Wood puppets. Meat puppets. Hand puppets. Sock puppets. Finger puppets. Shadow puppets. Puppets made out of fruit and vegetables.

GLORIA. Uh huh. So, you actually remember being a piece of wood?

PINOCCHIO. It's all kind of a blur, but I do have this clear memory of watching my brothers being tossed into a fire one after the other and burned to death, and this maniac coming at me with an ax. The son of a bitch was going to make me into a table leg. Now you might say, well, if you're a piece of wood, and the alternative is to be thrown in the fire so somebody can boil a pot of beans, then it might not be such a bad thing to be a table leg. But, really, would you want to be a table leg? People kicking you all the time, carving their initials in you. Cats scratching you. Dogs peeing on you. It's really not much of a life.

GLORIA. Uh huh. Gee, look at the time. You know, I actually need to go home and water my, um, goldfish and –

PINOCCHIO. So I just start screaming bloody murder, as loud as I can. I was surprisingly good at this for a piece of wood. It's amazing what you can do when someone's coming at you with an ax. So I scream and I scream and I scream. And this stupid bastard must not have been used to hearing pieces of wood screaming at him, because he drops the ax on his foot, and then starts hopping around swearing and yelling "Holy shit. Holy shit. It's a haunted piece of wood." And the next thing I know, he's sold me to this old character named Geppetto who makes puppets.

GLORIA. Well, that's a really nice story, but you know, I left the dog home by himself, and he gets really lonely and starts howling and shitting on the furniture, and –

PINOCCHIO. And I thought this guy was going to have a stroke when he carved my eyes, because they started moving back and forth, following him around the room. And he says to me, "My son, why are you looking at me?" Which is a really stupid question. I mean, if he didn't want me looking at him, why did he give me eyes?

GLORIA. Excuse me, I'm sorry, I don't want to be rude, but, really, that just doesn't make any sense at all. You just told me this other guy was coming at you with an ax. But you didn't have any eyes then, right? You were just a piece of wood. So how could a piece of wood without any eyes see a guy coming at him with an ax, and scream without a mouth?

PINOCCHIO. Because, as you meat people never seem to understand, but all inanimate objects know, you don't need eyes to see, you don't need ears to hear, and you don't need a mouth to scream. The world is already going on inside your head before you even have a head. Everything is alive. Everything is connected. And everything is conscious in some degree or other. I was just, for some reason, a little more self aware than most inanimate objects. Consciousness is a kind of curse, really. It was like I was aware of what he was doing, when he was carving me. And the more he carved, the more conscious I became. And then, when Geppetto started carving my nose, it kept growing and growing, and he had to keep cutting the end off. And he shook his head and said. "Oh, my son, this is not a good sign. This means you're going to be a wicked boy, and a born liar." Well, maybe so. But then again, he was carving me in his own image, like God, which is probably why God doesn't like looking in the mirror while he's putting on his lipstick. God looks in the mirror and thinks, shit, I'm old. And look at the mess I made, carving those meat puppets in my image. They're foul tempered and vain and selfish and ugly, just like me. What was I thinking? And I've got to say, it really was kind of gratifying, giving this pathetic old geezer a hard time. When he carved my mouth, I laughed at him, and stuck out my tongue. When he carved my hands, I ripped off his wig. When he finished my feet, I kicked him in the balls. When he taught me to walk, I galloped out the door like a racehorse, and he had to hobble down the street after me, yelling, "Wait. Stop that puppet. Stop that puppet."

Until the cops stopped him and thought he was drunk. And he said, "No, officer, I'm not drunk. I just carved a puppet and he kicked me in the balls and ran away." So they dragged him off and put him in a straight jacket, and I was free. Free! I was free! Which was really exciting for about five minutes, until it occurred to me, all right, so what the hell am I supposed to do now? I'm a puppet, for Christ sake. Just how free can you really be if you're a puppet, walking alone down pitch black streets in the middle of the night when you have no idea where you're going or why you're here? And also, I was starting to get really hungry. I didn't know what to do. I'd never been hungry when I was just a piece of wood. Then I found an egg, but before I could figure out what to do with it, the shell cracked and a chicken crawled out and flew away. And I thought, how weird is that? I mean, here's this thing you find the street, it could be a stone or something, this perfectly self contained little world, and then suddenly it cracks open and a bird flies out. How the hell did it get in there? And how did it know to break the shell, or how to fly? I didn't even know chickens could fly. But the chicken inside the egg is an allegory of the soul trapped in the body. It's God dropping a clue that things are not what they seem. That there's stuff happening on the other side of the shell we don't know anything about until the egg cracks and it comes flying out. The body is a shell, and when it dies, the soul flies away.

GLORIA. That's actually kind of deep.

PINOCCHIO. No shit. And then, while I was still thinking about that chicken, there was this bolt of lighting, and a big crash of thunder, and the wind really started blowing, so I ran to the nearest house and pounded on the door, to ask for shelter, or at least a piece of bread or something, and an old woman on the floor above the door opened up her window, and I thought, this is a kind person, she'll help me, and the old woman told me to shut the fuck up and then poured a whole pot full of piss all over me. And then it started pouring down rain, and I just ran and ran until I stepped in a pot hole and fell on my face, and then a cat came over and ate my feet. I don't know if a cat's ever eaten your feet before, but, trust me, it's a little discouraging, especially when you're covered in piss. And finally, I don't know how, I managed to crawl back to the toy shop. The door was still open, and there was no sign of Geppetto, but – you're not going to believe this –

GLORIA. Probably not.

PINOCCHIO. There was a talking cricket, crawling on the wall.

GLORIA. A talking cricket.

PINOCCHIO. I swear to God. It was a talking cricket.

GLORIA. Well, I didn't see that coming.

PINOCCHIO. Me neither. But this cricket told me he'd lived in that room for a hundred years, and acquired a lot of wisdom, and then he started giving me advice. I've just been carved out of a piece of wood, and then somebody poured a whole pot of piss all over me, and now this talking cricket is trying to lay some sort of great, spiritual truth on me, like he thinks he's revealing the secret of life, or something. And he's going on and on about wishes and stars and dreams or some sort of bullshit like that, but I was really in no mood to get a pep talk from some damned insect. So when he topped it off by suddenly bursting into song, that was it. I pulled a hammer off the work table and squashed him on the wall.

GLORIA. You squashed him on the wall?

PINOCCHIO. It made a hell of a mess, too.

GLORIA. You had a talking cricket who was trying to help you and because he started to sing a song you got a hammer and squashed him on the wall?

PINOCCHIO. Trust me, you should never start singing to somebody who's covered in piss and just had his feet gnawed off. Then Geppetto got back from his padded cell, where he finally convinced them he wasn't completely demented, and found me there on the floor. He was a little annoyed with me, for running away and getting him locked up and all, but he was a good natured old guy, and really lonesome, so he got me cleaned up and carved me a new pair of feet, and talking to me like I was his son. Which is kind of pathetic, but, then, when you get to be that age, you're desperate enough to love just about anything, I guess, and he didn't have the cricket to talk to any more, so I was pretty much all he had.

GLORIA. This is a really sad story.

PINOCCHIO. You're telling me. I felt so bad for this half senile old fart that in a moment of weakness I promised him I'd go to school, which made him so happy he went out and traded the only coat he had, in the middle of winter, for an old mouse eaten spelling book, and I thought, what the hell am I ever going to do with this stupid, smelly piece of crap, so on the way to school I sold it to some half wit and bought a ticket to a puppet show.

GLORIA. A puppet show?

PINOCCHIO. Well, I thought I could meet some other puppets. You know. Socialize with my own kind. Network. Schmooze.

GLORIA. But this poor old man gave up his only coat to get you a schoolbook, and you sold it and went to a puppet show?

PINOCCHIO. I'm beginning to sense a slightly judgmental tone in your voice. I hope you're not prejudiced against puppets. We need to have respect for all sorts of life, you know. Even talking pieces of wood. What you meat people don't seem to want to understand is that everything is haunted. Everything is alive. Everything is conscious. Children are born knowing this instinctively, but that knowledge is too disturbing to your pathetic egos, so you teach them to pretend it isn't true. But secretly you know there's something like a soul inside everything, like a little fragment of God, or Satan, or somebody. You don't want to believe that everything is alive because that means we can love like you and suffer like you.

GLORIA. You know what? I'm just going to go now.

PINOCCHIO. Why are you running away? What are you afraid of?

GLORIA. I'm not afraid of anything, I just think you and I are probably not, on the whole, a very good match. It's nothing personal.

PINOCCHIO. It's love, isn't it? You're deeply attracted to me and you're afraid of falling in love with a puppet.

GLORIA. I don't think that's it.

PINOCCHIO. No, you're right to be afraid. Love creates suffering for the lover and the beloved alike. Consciousness is a disease, and imagination dooms us all to a life of anguish, because if you can imagine that objects suffer, if you project this disease of consciousness upon objects, you awaken that consciousness in those objects, or at least your own awareness of it. And then you wonder, was it always there? Or did you create it? Or is it an illusion? But then if my consciousness an illusion, then maybe so is yours. And if consciousness is an illusion, then who's having the illusion? Are you hallucinating me? Or am I hallucinating you? Or is God hallucinating both of us?

GLORIA. You see, this is the problem. I don't know what the hell you're talking about.

PINOCCHIO. Maybe God is having an elaborate series of illusions and it's driven him insane. He's brought us to life the same way he or she was brought to life by the imagination of some other loony God. But to give things consciousness, or to awaken the illusion of consciousness in objects is evil because it creates suffering where there was only nothing. If you imagine that objects are conscious you project feelings upon them and then get attached to them and suffer, because the more imagination you have, the more love you feel and so the more you suffer because everything you love is mortal, like you, and will, eventually, like you, inevitably be destroyed.

GLORIA. This is getting way, way too deep for me. All I was looking for this evening was a nice plate of spaghetti and meatballs and a glass of wine. I didn't order a wheelbarrow full of philosophical bullshit about puppets. So thank you for the unusual evening. I'll just get a cab.

(She starts to go, but he jumps up and grabs her arms.)

PINOCCHIO. Can't you hear all the agony around you? All of us objects are alive, and we're all watching you. At night, while you're sleeping, we move around in your house, your dishes and spoons and the salt and pepper shakers and your shoes and gloves and clocks, dancing and singing and playing the banjo. And some night we're going to creep into your room like rats and tie you up and pour salt in your ears and gnaw out your throat.

GLORIA. Could you let go of my arms, please? Just let go of my arms, okay?

PINOCCHIO. When I ran away from home, do you know what I found? Fakes. Fakes everywhere. I met a blind cat and a lame fox, hobbling along together, and they were both faking. Everybody is faking. A white blackbird tried to warn me, but the cat ate him. And I've been hallucinating the voice of the talking cricket. Don't listen to bad companions, he says. The problem is, all companions are bad. Come with us to the Land of Owls, the fox said. In the Land of Owls there is a Magic Field. You dig a hole, put your money in, cover it up. Pee on it. Add salt. Go to sleep. When you wake up, you'll have a money tree with gold pieces on it like apples. And I believed them. I actually believed them. We're like sheep, running off a cliff.

GLORIA. Could somebody help me here? Waiter? Waiter?

PINOCCHIO. I'm so lonely. I lost something in the woods and now I can't remember what it was. Every time I see an oak tree, I think, is that my mother? I will die of loneliness and four black rabbits will carry my coffin. And yet I was loved once. Can you believe that?

GLORIA. No.

PINOCCHIO. A blue haired fairy loved me. But I ran off to the Inn of the Red Crayfish, where they stuff themselves with rabbits and lizards, and told her I was coming back but I never did and she died of grief. Puppets abandon everybody. And we're all puppets here. Welcome to the Great Puppet Theatre. Now and then God throws a puppet into the fire to cook his mutton. You never know when it might be you. He has an enormous beard and smells like a chicken coop. I see the dead girl with blue hair everywhere I go, and I hear the cricket singing in my head. We're like souls trapped in a fishing net. I've been swallowed by a fish. Turned into a donkey.

GLORIA. Will you just take your stupid puppet hands off of me? Jesus. You try to have a pleasant evening with a nice guy and you end up with a puppet who thinks he was turned into a donkey. Isn't there a nice, normal guy somewhere in the world? Why do I always end up with weirdos and losers? The last one wanted to photograph my elbows. The one before that thought he'd been abducted and molested by squirrels. And another guy thought he was Rumpelstiltskin. Are all men insane?

Or am I insane for still looking for one? I've got to get the hell out of this place.

PINOCCHIO. No. Wait. Please don't go. Please. I'll let go of your arm, right now. I swear. But please just wait a minute. Okay?

GLORIA. Okay.

(He lets go of her arm. She hesitates.)

PINOCCHIO. I'm really sorry. I got a little worked up. I didn't mean to scare you. This is what always happens. The problem is, I can't lie. I mean, I can lie, but when I do, my nose starts to grow. And people don't want to hear the truth, so I hold it in as long as I can, but sooner or later it just comes pouring out. And the thing about the truth is, when it all comes pouring out at once, like horses stampeding out of a burning barn, it scares people so much they prefer to think I'm crazy because people don't want the truth. They always prefer a comforting lie. All they want is puppet shows.

GLORIA. I don't want any goddamned puppet shows. I want something real. Somebody real.

PINOCCHIO. Only until you get it. Look at my nose. Am I lying? Am I?

GLORIA. I'm going now. Don't try to follow me. Don't follow me, and don't call me. I'm throwing my phone in the toilet. Christ, I'm going to start dating women.

(She goes.)

PINOCCHIO. *(Calling after her.)* I know I'm a little different. But there's some good things about me. I'm always hard. Think about that. I'm made of wood, so I'm always hard. All the time. Who else do you know who can say that? Huh? Hello?

(Pause.)

I wanted to be a real boy, and here I am. It's always the same. Lie and your nose grows. Tell the truth and they hate you. And when the Puppet Master throws you on the fire, all you can do is burn. And the other puppets, your brothers, will not save you. Nobody can save you. Because puppets have wooden heads and no heart. Just like people. And puppets never grow. They are born puppets, live the lives of puppets, and die puppets. The truth doesn't make you free. It isolates you and then it kills you.

(Pause.)

I miss that damned cricket.

(The light fades on him and goes out.)

Rusalka

A Play

by Don Nigro

CHARACTERS

ROSSI – a police detective
LYDIA – a young woman

SETTING

Two wooden chairs and a wooden table. Light above.
Darkness around them.

(**ROSSI** *is questioning* **LYDIA**. *There is an overhead light above a wooden table.* **LYDIA** *sits in a wooden chair at the table,* **ROSSI** *sitting across from her.*)

LYDIA. She's a little bit crazy. She talks to mirrors. I comforted her when she was afraid. There are monsters everywhere, she said. When we played Casino she'd talk to the face cards. They all had different personalities. You're only a pack of cards, she said. And then, whispering in my ear, Dodgson was a pervert. She said God lived in the subterranean passages below the house and raised sheep, but he very seldom came up any more because it was too depressing. She could play "Danube Waves" on the accordion. Ivanovici. But she didn't do it very often, out of respect for other people's sanity, because some music was designed by the Devil to drive people crazy if they listened to it too much. One morning she found cloven footprints in the snow around the house. She said the Devil was after her. Once we went into a toy shop. It was night and very cold and it was snowing. There was a red lamp above the door. She would stare into the eyes of the dolls and try to communicate telepathically with them. We walked home through the cemetery and somebody had knocked off all the heads of the angels on the monuments. The Devil's getting closer, she said. She could sit and watch the moon for hours. She was trying to catch it moving. We used to wash ourselves together. She had the most perfect body. Once she washed her feet in ginger ale. She said it tickled.

ROSSI. Was she seeing anybody?

LYDIA. She'd go to bars and pick up these awful men. I warned her about this Russian guy, but she liked him.

He has wild eyes, she said. One night he dragged her all the way across the parking lot by her hair. I shot him in the ass with a BB gun. And when he came for me I shot him in the face and he ran away. He moved to Texas after that.

ROSSI. Do you have any idea where she might have gone?

LYDIA. There was this place in the woods she went where mushrooms would come up after rain, and there was a little patch of ferns, on the other side of the hill, and if you stood very still, you could hear bees buzzing, where there weren't any bees, and see this stand of maple trees moving, when there wasn't any wind, and the hackles on the back of your neck would rise, and you could feel him.

ROSSI. Feel who?

LYDIA. The great god Pan. He lives in the woods. But that's just an alias. He's really the Devil. Sometimes we'd sneak into old abandoned houses to look for the ghosts. She said every place is full of ghosts, and everything is synchronicity, and the most interesting parts are the mistakes. She was interested in the archetypal connections between creative thought and the subconscious. She said the world was a forest of mystical symbols. That everything was full of gods. And that Kepler murdered Tycho Brahe.

ROSSI. Who is this?

LYDIA. Kepler the astronomer. Murdered Tycho Brahe, his mentor. So that then he, Kepler, would then be the greatest astronomer in the world. She said we murder the people we love, either by accident or on purpose. Tycho Brahe had an artificial nose. Syphilis, I think. His nose just fell off one day. So he had another nose made. But it was brass, or something.

ROSSI. When was the last time you saw her?

LYDIA. Last night. In my dream. We were somewhere in the marshes. Bogs. Romney Marsh. Or New Jersey. There was fog everywhere. And there was this creature. I don't know what it was. It had these long arms. And it was reaching up and putting its hands around her ankles. That's all I remember.

ROSSI. I'm not talking about your dreams. I mean when was the last time you actually saw her in real life?

LYDIA. Dreams are real life. They're just real life that hasn't happened yet.

ROSSI. She didn't mention that she was thinking of leaving town?

LYDIA. Timoshenko.

ROSSI. What?

LYDIA. That was the Russian guy's name. That moved to Texas to work on oil rigs. He smelled like my grandfather's basement.

ROSSI. Do you think she might have gone to see him?

LYDIA. No. She could only live in places where it rains.

ROSSI. Did she have any family?

LYDIA. She said the Devil ate them all. She told me she came from East Mars.

ROSSI. Pennsylvania?

LYDIA. No. The planet Mars. She wasn't serious. It was a literary reference. They asked this poet where his poems came from, and he said poetry comes from East Mars. He meant you can't force it to happen. It comes to you from this other place. She was from some other place. The banks of the Danube, or some other river somewhere. And she was like a poem. Once she woke up in the middle of the night and sat up in bed and said, All day it rained the Devil's blood. And then she went back to sleep. We sometimes slept in the same bed. She was afraid of the dark. So I'd hold her. The Russian guy called her Rusalka. The rusalka is a Russian fairy girl, a nymph who lives in the water like a mermaid but also sometimes in the trees in the woods and lures men to their destruction, tangles them in her long, red hair and drowns them, or sometimes tickles them to death. But she said, no. I am not her anymore. I am somebody else now. I've been out of the water too long. If you go to the woods and stand very still and listen, she said, you can hear the Devil whispering. The Russian guy had a point. She didn't seem entirely human. She came with a sense of strangeness.

ROSSI. Had she ever been in a mental institution?

LYDIA. I don't know.

ROSSI. Have you?

LYDIA. Not that I can remember. Have you?

ROSSI. Do you have a photograph of her?

LYDIA. She never wanted her picture taken. She said it wouldn't come out. Are you married?

ROSSI. What do you think happened to her?

LYDIA. She saw too deep, and too much. And what she saw was chaos. That was from a book, too, I think. One morning she opened her eyes and said, Chaos. I've awakened in chaos. I liked to watch her sleep. But she had bad dreams. She was dating some other guy. But I never met him. Maybe he's the person you should be talking to.

ROSSI. Lydia.

LYDIA. What? You have very sad eyes. Like you've seen something you want to forget.

ROSSI. Did you kill her?

LYDIA. Did I kill her?

ROSSI. Did you?

LYDIA. Why would I kill her? Why on earth would you ask me a question like that?

ROSSI. Well, for one thing, when you came in here, you were completely covered in blood.

LYDIA. It was the Devil's blood. Last night it rained the Devil's blood.

ROSSI. I don't think so.

LYDIA. Oh, yes. We went out naked and danced in the rain.

ROSSI. And then what happened? Something happened. What was it? Did she tell you she was going to Texas, to be with the Russian?

LYDIA. No. She didn't want him any more. She liked this other guy.

ROSSI. Maybe you had a quarrel about it. You were drinking and you went out dancing naked in the rain and she told you she was leaving and you tried to stop her and maybe you pushed her, and she fell and hit her head. Was it something like that?

LYDIA. No. It was nothing like that.

ROSSI. Then what was it like? Where did you put her, Lydia?

LYDIA. I didn't put her anywhere. She's a rusalka. You can't kill her. Although sometimes they die of grief. Mostly they break other people's hearts, but sometimes, on very rare occasions, the rusalka will actually fall in love herself, and if she's not loved in return, she'll die. But that's not what happened.

ROSSI. What did happen, then?

LYDIA. You're not fooling me, you know. I know who you are.

ROSSI. What do you mean?

LYDIA. You want me to believe you're just some random police detective, but I know. I can see through your disguise.

ROSSI. I'm not wearing a disguise.

LYDIA. Everybody's wearing a disguise. And you have a really good one. But I can see through it. She taught me.

ROSSI. If I'm not a police detective, then who am I?

LYDIA. You know who you are.

ROSSI. No. I've forgotten who I am. Tell me.

LYDIA. You're the Devil.

ROSSI. I'm the Devil?

LYDIA. She could smell you. Prowling round and round the house at night. She could smell your blood in the rain. He's very close now, she said. Hold me. He's very close, and he's coming for me now. I can smell brimstone in the rain. And so I held her. There in the rain. And all around us the Devil's blood rained down. Why do you hate her so much?

ROSSI. I don't hate her. I don't even know her. I'm just trying to find out what happened to her.

LYDIA. I'll tell you what I think. The Devil hates a rusalka who falls in love. And he hunts her down because she's betrayed him. Because there is no love in Hell.

ROSSI. That's not true.

LYDIA. I think it is.

ROSSI. No. There is love in Hell. In fact, Hell is made entirely of love. Love is the most terrible punishment there is. It's the suffering that lasts for all eternity. You're never going to see her again. That's your punishment.

LYDIA. And yours is that she doesn't love you. You see? I can see it on your face. I can see it in your eyes. You're the other guy she was seeing. You were walking around our house all night, looking in the windows. I saw your cloven footprints in the snow. You want her but you can't have her. Your punishment is that she doesn't love you. She doesn't love you. She loves me. She only loves me. And I'll never tell you where she's gone. No matter what you do to me, I'll never tell. I'll never tell.

(Pause.)

So come on. Do something to me. Do something.

(Pause.)

I dare you.

(They look at each other. The light fades on them and goes out.)

Humpty Dumpty

A Play

by Don Nigro

CHARACTERS

HUMPTY DUMPTY – a large, round person, shaped rather like an egg, sitting on a wall.

"When *I* use a word," Humpty Dumpty said, in rather a scornful tone, "it means just what I choose it to mean – neither more nor less."

"The question is," said Alice, "whether you *can* make words mean so many different things."

"The question is," said Humpty Dumpty, "which is to be master – that's all."

– Lewis Carroll, *Through The Looking Glass*

(**HUMPTY DUMPTY**, *a large egg shaped person, sitting on a wall.*)

HUMPTY DUMPTY. One of the central elements in my plan to make The Other Side Of The Looking Glass great again is the construction of this magnificent wall, and I am very pleased to celebrate the completion of the first thirty-seven and a half feet of it today. I want to thank you all for coming. I understand this is the biggest crowd in history to ever come to the opening of a thirty-seven and a half foot wall by a large egg, and I'm very proud of that, and I know that we all feel much, much safer now.

I do want to emphasize, believe me, that I have absolutely nothing against good, honest, hard working rabbits coming to Wonderland legally, although of course I continue to strongly believe that preference must be given to rabbits who can contribute significantly to our way of life, chiefly White Rabbits, preferably Norwegian or from some place like that, where they do clog dancing and make butter. Everybody knows that I am the least prejudiced egg on this side of the Looking Glass, but experience has demonstrated that rabbits who come from rabbit shit holes bring those shit holes with them when they get here, along with all their shit hole relatives who make really smelly food that gives me indigestion and makes me fart, and a lot of incredibly annoying music. Believe me, and I think I can speak for all decent people when I say this, we don't need that sort of rabbits here. We've already wasted far too much time having to exterminate the rabbits who were already here when we got here, where of course we have always been and always will be, because God gave us this country, and I expect you all to stand up and cheer when I say that, otherwise you're all traitors, off with your heads. Just kidding, folks. Well, kind of. At least for now.

I understand that some people were concerned, when I was hoisted up here by that fork lift, that I might fall off this wall. Let me assure you that I am, believe me, in no danger whatsoever of falling off anything. I have the best balance in the world. My personal physician has certified that I am the most perfectly balanced egg in the observable universe. This is a matter of public knowledge. And if by some chance I should ever fall, which of course will never happen, the White King, who is a very good friend of mine, has promised me, with his very own mouth, and a very pretty mouth it is, too – the White King himself has personally assured me not to worry, that all of his horses and all of his men, in the unlikely event that it should become necessary, will be perfectly capable of putting me back together gain.

I have, as you may know, a very cordial working relationship with the White King, since for some years now it has been my great honor and privilege to wash his money, because money – a lot of people don't know this – money can get quite dirty, as it moves from one place to another, and the White King and various members of his court have an awful lot of dirty money to take care of, which it is my great honor and privilege to be able to wash for them. And I want to add that I am shocked, shocked to hear that anybody would suggest that there is anything wrong with this. Anybody who thinks that should be ashamed of himself. After all, Wonderland was mostly constructed with dirty money, a fact that I'm very proud of.

And you can take me at my word. Because I have a lot of words. I have the best words of anybody. And when I use a word, it means exactly what I choose it to mean. Anyway, the question is not what things mean. The question is who is to be master. That's all. It's not that complicated. Everything is not a riddle. Everything is a game. And the point of the game is to win. The rules don't really matter. Rules don't apply to winners. And only winning matters.

Excuse me. Excuse me. I'm talking here. No, I'm talking now. And I'm not taking any questions from that uppity Alice person. I love women, believe me, and I have great respect for them, I really do, but honestly, why can't they learn to just shut the hell up once in a while? It's very unattractive, always jabbering away with all these questions and criticisms. Am I right, men? Am I right? Alice, you're an ugly little girl. Go home. Nobody wants to hear your stupid comments. Could somebody just remove her now? Could the lizards just take her out of here? If she gives you any trouble, just punch her in the face. Punch her right in the face. Thank you. Thank you very much. This is why we need a wall, folks. To keep people like that out. Traitors. TRAITORS. TRAITORS.

And this is just the beginning, folks. We're going to develop Wonderland. We're going to pave over that checkerboard and make this place start paying. We're digging treacle wells and reopening the tart mines and –

Oh, shit. Who am I kidding? Just who do I think I'm kidding? There's nobody here. I'm talking to myself on top of this stupid wall in the middle of nowhere and nobody's listening. It's lonely at the top. I'm feeling kind of dizzy. It could be those little blue pills. I might have taken too many with my Diet Pepsi. Maybe this is all just a bad dream. I have a lot of bad dreams. Sometimes I dream I'm falling, from an enormous height, a very tall building, the top of a massively tall wall, or from Heaven. I don't know. But I'm falling, and it's terrifying, and all I can think about is what's going to happen when I finally hit bottom. If there is a bottom. Somebody told me once that when God threw Satan out of Heaven, he fell for a million years, before he finally landed in Hell. And in my dream sometimes I fall and fall until I realize I'm beginning to feel intense heat rising up from below, and I think, either that's Hell down there, or God is making an omelet. He's making an omelet. God's making an omelet. I don't want to be God's omelet. Why can't he have corn flakes? WHY CAN'T HE JUST GO TO THE WAFFLE HOUSE LIKE A NORMAL PERSON?

All right. Calm down, Humpty. Don't get hysterical. Take a deep breath. You're safe. You're on your wall. Nobody can get you while you're on your wall. Unless they've got cross bows. Or automatic weapons. Or rocks.

Wait a minute. Am I turned around? Which side is our side? I'm confused. Is the wall supposed to keep them out from that way or that way? Oh, my God. I can't tell. And my butt hurts. Don't look down. Don't look down. I never should have had those enchiladas. Damned foreigners.

I'm so confused. I'm a stranger here myself. Have I always been on this wall? I don't know where I came from. Were my parents eggs? Or was I laid by a giant chicken? Did God lay me? Is God a giant chicken? I don't know who I am. I don't know who I am. I don't know who I am.

No. It's all right. This is just a dream. I'm just a character in a nursery rhyme in a dream. Humpty Dumpty jumped over the moon. No, that's not it.

Wait. What's that? What's that strange dark shape, flapping up there? Is that some sort of – is that what ate Tweedledum and Tweedledee? Is it some kind of giant bird thing? Is it the Jabberwock? Mother? Is that you, Mother? I think it is.

(Sound of the screeching of a giant bird from above, and a great shadow across the stage. Raising his arms to heaven in wonder.)

It's God. It's God. It's God, in the form of a gigantic bird. God has come to give me my just reward! GOD HAS COME TO TAKE ME TO THE WAFFLE HOUSE. I'M SAVED. I'M SAVED. I'M –

(Losing his balance, waving his arms above him, he falls over backwards on the other side of the wall.)

AHHHHHHHHHHHHHHHHHHHHHH.

(Sound of an enormous splat. Blackout.)

Brimstone Run

A Play

by Don Nigro

CHARACTERS

BUBBER ROOKS – a man of twenty-five, who runs a junkyard by the dump.

SETTING

The junkyard by the dump up Shite Creek near Brimstone Run just outside Armitage, a small town in east Ohio.

TIME

Some time around 1856.

*(**BUBBER ROOKS** speaks to us from his house by the junkyard, late at night.)*

BUBBER ROOKS. I don't know exactly what come over me. Well, I know what come over me, but I don't know why. Well, I know why, but –

Shit. I just wanted her sister. I had my wife and I wanted her sister. I don't know what it was about her. I think maybe if she hadn't been her sister I might not have looked twice at her. I mean, I married the pretty one and then I wanted the other one. You get what you want, that's a curse because what the hell do you do then? You want something else. And I wanted my wife's sister. I knew it was wrong. Even out here at the junkyard by the dump we're not animals. Well, we are animals, but no more than rich people are animals. Rich people are just animals with money and better haircuts.

So I fought it. You can't say I didn't fight it, because I did. Well, what I did was, I drank. And that didn't really help much, but it beat not drinking, so I drank some more. And before long I was the damnedest falling down drunk you ever met in your life. Ran into the mirror and cracked it all the way from one side to the other and dislocated my nose.

Also, I slept with my wife. Every time I heard the Devil whispering in my ear I'd fornicate with my wife and try not to think about her sister. But from the front I was too close to see her clearly and from the back they could have been twins. And after a while no matter how hard I tried not to I was giving it to my wife and thinking about her sister. It was almost as good as a threesome. Especially after her sister come to live with us after Dolly got pregnant, and the walls in this house is as thin as a bed slat, and Dolly would make these noises when I did it to her, sort of like a pig squealing, like WHEEEEEEEEEEEEEEEEEEK! WHEEEEEEEEEEEEEEK! Sorta like that, only louder. And I actually think having her sister in the next room about four feet away on the other side of the blue carnation wall paper every night probably just made her squeal louder, like, Listen to me, sister. Listen to me squeal. I got a man and you don't.

I don't want to suggest that Dolly was a mean person, because she wasn't a mean person at all. Or that she didn't love her sister, because Dolly loved Aggie just fine. They'd always been close. I mean, they seemed close. Well, they was women, so what the hell did I know? But whatever was going on there in her head – and my experience is you don't ever want to get too sure you know what's going on inside a woman's head, because whatever the hell you think it is, trust me, pal, either you are wrong, or you're going to wish you was, but whatever she was thinking, the more pregnant she got, the more I wanted to diddle her, and the more I diddled her, the louder she'd squeal, and knowing her sister was just on the other side of the wall just did something to me I can't even describe. I was like a maniac. I just couldn't stop. I was so damned tense that right in the middle of doing it I'd get these awful leg cramps, sometimes in both legs, and I don't know if you've ever had double leg cramps or not but ordinarily that might have distracted me a bit from the fornication, but even if I'd wanted to take a moment for my calf muscles and my thigh muscles to unclench, I couldn't have, because Dolly, she had her legs wrapped around me like a possum on a stick, so we just kept going, me screaming from pain like AAAAAAAHHHHHHH, AHHHHHHHHHHHH, and her squealing like a pig, WHEEEEEEEEEK! WHEEEEEEEEEEEK! Lord, it must have sounded to her sister like the fricking Spanish Inquisition in there.

Dolly was actually kind of an unusual girl. Her mother always said she was a little bit fey. She'd have dreams about people that would come true just often enough to keep you off balance. She used to wake up screaming at night sometimes when we was first married, dreaming she was falling and falling, all the way down to Hell. My brother Jackson used to say, Dolly might be fey, but Bubber is just plain nuts. Dolly was only ten years old when Jackson went off to the Mexican War and she cried like a baby when he left. And also he never come back. John Pendragon told us he just turned around one day and Jackson was gone. I still dream about him sometimes, wandering around like a ghost somewhere in Mexico. Sometimes you even miss people who treated you like dirt. Families are like that.

When I was a little boy, Jackson used to tell me that the Devil lived out by the Indian Caves, near that spring where Brimstone Run starts. And whenever him or Daddy would beat on me, I'd go out to Brimstone Run and sit, in a place where a long time ago old man Schmidt or somebody or other had dug a whole bunch of big deep holes to mine some damn thing or other. That was the place where I could hear the voices the best, the ones that whispered in my head. You could hear them gurgling there in the water. I figured it was the Devil whispering to me. Which scared the hell out of me, but also I felt like he had something important to tell me. Although I could never figure out what the hell it was.

Anyway, with all that nonstop copulating going on every night, before long Dolly was, like they say in the Good Book, great with child. And that's an understatement. Dolly was a bitty little person, but man was she great with child. She looked like she'd swallowed the moon. And she was just a little bit cranky and uncomfortable after almost nine months of getting bigger and bigger, and I was drinking pretty heavy, and one night I went up the steps and walked into the wrong bedroom and there was her sister Aggie standing there stark naked.

Well, I just froze. I absolutely could not move. And neither could Aggie. The two of us stood there staring at each other for I don't know how long. And then out waddles Dolly from the other bedroom and sees me standing there with her naked sister and then she kind of just exploded like a fire cracker in a water melon. She starts screaming bloody murder at me, and I'm trying to explain that it's an accident, except I don't think a woman who's nine months' pregnant wants to hear a man talking about accidents, and I'm moving towards her and she's backing up to get away from me and then her water breaks. And there's water or some damned kind of a mess all over the floor, and I reach for her to help her and she keeps backing up and she slips in the wet and falls backwards and there she goes, tumbling down the staircase backwards. And the next thing I know she's laying at the bottom of the steps and she's not moving and Aggie has run down the steps naked and I'm just standing there looking down at them like it's all a bad dream. And by the time we got their brother Scooter to run and fetch Doc McGort all the way out here to the dump I had a baby boy and Dolly was dead.

We called him Egg, because Dolly had made me promise if it was a boy we'd name him after her Uncle Egbert who used to raise turtles, but I thought Egbert was a stupid name, so we called him Egg, which is also a stupid name but which is at least shorter, so it's not stupid for quite so long while you're saying it. And Aggie took care of him, and she consoled me for my loss, and I consoled her, and one thing led to another, and I ended up marrying her, and we had two little girls, Tootsie and Koralee, but here's the thing: every night I kept dreaming about Dolly. All that time I was married to her I was thinking about her sister, and now that I was married to her sister, every time we did it I thought about Dolly. I was in love with a dead girl I'd pretty much killed because I wanted her sister and now that I was married to the sister all I could think about was Dolly.

So I went back to drinking, partly because if I just had enough to drink I could almost forget which one I was doing it to. And one night I got to feeling really bad so I got extremely drunk and walked out towards Brimstone Run and I could hear them voices whispering in my head, the Devil or somebody, I don't know, but I couldn't quite make out what they was trying to say, and I got so distracted I stepped into one of them holes at the quarry where somebody or other had mined something fifty years ago and fell and landed at the bottom like a broken toy. And I was laying at the bottom of that hole, with my neck all twisted funny, and I couldn't feel much of anything, and I looked up at the sky, and I saw this big old moon looking down at me, and then a little face looked over the side of the hole, and I saw it was my little boy, Egg, who was five years old then, looking down at me, and I thought, this is how my son is going to remember his daddy: laying all twisted up like a rag doll at the bottom of a hole. And then I died.

And ever since I been dead, I been running over and over in my brain everything that happened. And I got to come to the conclusion it must all have happened for a reason. I don't know what the hell that reason would be, but it must mean something. It couldn't mean nothing. Because that would mean that nothing means anything. Not that I think anything means anything. But just the fact that a person wants it to mean something ought to mean something, don't it?

Because here in my dream, which is what being dead feels like, Dolly is here, and she follows me around, all up and down Brimstone Run, and keeps wanting to have sex. More and more sex. It's driving me crazy. I didn't know dead people could have sex. I thought maybe they played canasta or something. But the thing is, when I make love to Dolly, here in Heaven or Hell or whatever the heck this place is, I only think about her now, but every now and then right in the middle of me doing it to her Dolly yells out, "Jackson. Jackson." Which is more than a little bit disturbing on several levels. But what I'm not sure about is whether she's really thinking about my brother when I'm doing it to her, or is she just yelling that out to get back and me for thinking about her sister and pushing her down the stairs. So I try to just forget about all that and think about her sister. But I can't even hardly remember her sister.

What I do remember, all the time, is my little boy, his little head, looking down into that hole, and seeing this person who looks like a broken doll at the bottom of the hole, and thinking, yes, that's my father. That's him. That's the fella that told me the Devil lives out at Brimstone Run. And I wonder when he grows up and makes love to his wife, who's he going to be thinking about? And who's he going to kill? Because I think that's probably the only true thing I ever taught my little boy, through the object lesson of my life: the only true thing about love is that it kills somebody sooner or later.

But I still hear those voices. And what they whisper at me now is that death is a dream. And if death is a dream, then I want to wake up now. I want to wake up.

(The light fades on him and goes out.)

Nictzin Dyalhis

A Play

by Don Nigro

CHARACTERS

HARRIET
NICTZIN

SETTING

Two pools of light on an otherwise dark stage.

AUTHOR'S NOTES

Nictzin Dyalhis (1873-1942) was an author of fantastic stories for *Weird Tales* and other pulp magazines, among them "When The Green Star Waned," "The Sapphire Goddess," and "The Sea Witch." He had one eye, was half Welsh and half Guatemalan, had an Aztec first name, and died a recluse somewhere near the Maryland shore. His wife is said to have spent some years in a mental institution. This play is probably about somebody else.

*(Sound of the ocean. **HARRIET** and **NICTZIN**, in two pools of light, on an otherwise dark stage.)*

HARRIET. I know why you go out there every night.

NICTZIN. You don't know.

HARRIET. You're waiting for her.

NICTZIN. I'm just walking.

HARRIET. I've heard you talking in your sleep.

NICTZIN. You're dreaming.

HARRIET. I know when I'm dreaming.

NICTZIN. I don't think so.

HARRIET. Do you know when you're dreaming?

NICTZIN. Am I dreaming now?

HARRIET. You dream about her every night.

NICTZIN. I can't control what I dream.

HARRIET. She's out there in the ocean, waiting for you.

NICTZIN. This is a fantasy.

HARRIET. Your fantasies are more real to you than I am.

NICTZIN. That's not true.

HARRIET. You don't know what's true.

NICTZIN. I need to go.

HARRIET. You need to go. You need to go away. You're always going away. Even when you're here, you're someplace else. You and those *Weird Tales* people. Those people. Why do you write for those people?

NICTZIN. Because they pay me.

HARRIET. Sometimes they pay you. Never enough. But don't you see that it's evil?

NICTZIN. It's not evil. It's just stories.

HARRIET. Stories are evil. Look what they've done to you.

NICTZIN. They haven't done anything to me.

HARRIET. I'm losing you. I know I'm losing you to her. She lures you out there, to walk every night by the ocean, because she wants you. She wants your soul.

NICTZIN. Nobody wants my soul. There's nobody out there.

HARRIET. Liar.

NICTZIN. I'm not a liar. I'm a writer.

HARRIET. Writer.

NICTZIN. You need to calm down.

HARRIET. I don't want to calm down.

NICTZIN. They'll come and give you a sedative if you don't calm down.

HARRIET. I don't want their medicine. It's horrible. I can't think straight. Listen to me. I know. I know better than you because I can see. I can see her. I can look with a clear eye. Your vision is clouded by lust. You go out on the shore and walk at night and look at the ocean and wait for her. The people in town think you're just a crazy old man. They call you One Eyed Jack. They don't know who you are.

NICTZIN. I don't know who I am.

HARRIET. Half Welsh and half Guatemalan with an Aztec first name and one eye and they write you all those creepy fan letters and make up weird stories about you and think they know you, all those crazy, pathetic *Weird Tales* people who have no lives and think your stories about other dimensions and other realities are more real than their own ridiculous lives, or my ridiculous life. Your stories are sexy and strange and your name is strange and you never write back to any of them and then you let those comic book people steal your ideas –

NICTZIN. Nobody stole anything.

HARRIET. They get rich and you live in a shack alone by the ocean with all this darkness in your head waiting for her to come out of the ocean naked and get you while I'm trapped here in this horrible place with all these crazy people.

NICTZIN. It was for the best.

HARRIET. It was not for the best. Whose best? Maybe yours. Maybe hers. Not mine.

NICTZIN. I didn't know what else to do.

HARRIET. You put me in here so you could be with her. She's what you want. You dream about her and she makes love to you while you sleep. You think she loves you, but that's all an illusion. She's going to drown you out there. You'll be just another human sacrifice. Nictzin. You've got to listen to me.

NICTZIN. Go away.

HARRIET. Nictzin Dyalhis.

NICTZIN. Leave me alone.

HARRIET. She calls you in the night.

NICTZIN. I need to go.

HARRIET. She dances naked for you in your head.

NICTZIN. She's calling me.

HARRIET. Strawberry blonde in green light.

NICTZIN. I can hear her.

HARRIET. Nictzin.

NICTZIN. Listen.

HARRIET. Nictzin Dyalhis.

NICTZIN. Can you hear that?

HARRIET. Nictzin. Nictzin Dyalhis.

NICTZIN. She's calling me.

HARRIET. Well, go to her, then.

NICTZIN. She wants me.

HARRIET. You poor fool.

NICTZIN. I can hear her.

HARRIET. Didn't you know?

NICTZIN. I've got to go out to the ocean.

HARRIET. Didn't you know that all the while it was me?

NICTZIN. Out there in the ocean.

HARRIET. All the while it was me.

(The light fades on them and goes out.)

www.ingramcontent.com/pod-product-compliance
Lightning Source LLC
Chambersburg PA
CBHW072008290426
44109CB00018B/2178